# Praise for *Give Me Five!* . . .

*Through the five collaborations featured in this resource, schools in Pampa Independent School District experienced significant, sustainable gains in student achievement. Here's what some of them had to say.*

I have never seen so much excitement among my teachers about teaching math. I enjoy hearing the teachers and the math coach talking about what the lesson is going to be about. Then, I enjoy going into the classroom and observing and watching the students learn from each other. It helps me to know how it all fits together.

> —Jill Faubion, principal

With so many students it's hard to get to every kid and hear their thinking. Having a math coach and a principal in my classroom is a great help; they are extra ears and eyes to see things and hear things from my students that I don't always hear.

> —Kristie Troxell, kindergarten teacher

You always want to be careful of not pinning one more thing on teachers. These collaborations are not something else to do; they're learning. They're all about the teachers continuing their learning to make sure they are meeting the needs of their students. It's a collaborative process of putting together good structures and strategies and understanding the math behind the math. This is the most powerful thing—getting those collaborative structures in place.

> –Evan Smith, deputy superintendent

The Shared Classroom Experience helps everyone to be equal partners. It is not a hierarchal relationship. Everyone has an equal voice, and everyone's voice is heard. Everybody comes in with the shared goal of listening to student thinking, collecting student strategies, and figuring out how can we work together to move toward student success.

> –Courtney Blackmon, math coach

I now know a lot more about the power of questioning. In the past I may have heard a student's answer and not probed and asked them more questions: why are you thinking this? Why did you choose this strategy? Collaborating with our math coach has helped me find out more about what a student is thinking—really dig deep and find out what strategy they used and why they came to the answer they did.

> —Erin Easley, fifth-grade teacher

We have seen improvements in our math program from our lowest level to our highest level. We've become more collaborative. Just to hear the conversations that our teachers now have; they're so much deeper and so much richer than they were prior to this work.

> –Barry Haenisch, superintendent

Any teacher who has an opportunity to peer teach with another teacher should jump at that opportunity. Whether it's the same grade level or a different grade level, two heads are always better than one!

> —Laurie Lance, first-grade teacher

# Give Me Five!

## Five Coach–Teacher–Principal Collaborations
### That Promote Mathematics Success

A Multimedia Professional Learning Resource

## Janice Bradley • Dana Cargill

**Includes
Video Streaming**

**Math Solutions**
Sausalito, California, USA

**Math Solutions**
One Harbor Drive, Suite 101
Sausalito, California, USA 94965
www.mathsolutions.com

**Library of Congress Cataloging-in-Publication Data**

Names: Bradley, Janice. | Cargill, Dana.
Title: Give me five! : five coach-teacher-principal collaborations that
promote mathematics success : a multimedia professional learning resource
/ Janice Bradley, Dana Cargill.
Description: Sausalito, California, USA : Math Solutions, [2017] | Includes
bibliographical references and index.
Identifiers: LCCN 2017014034 | ISBN 9781935099390 (pbk.)
Subjects: LCSH: Mathematics—Study and teaching—United States. | Mathematics
teachers—In-service training—United States. | Teachers—In-service
training—United States. | Teacher effectiveness—United States. |
Teachers—Professional relationships—United States.
Classification: LCC QA13 .B73 2017 | DDC 510.71/073—dc23
LC record available at https://lccn.loc.gov/2017014034

ISBN-13: 978-1-935099-39-0
ISBN-10: 1-935099-39-6

Math Solutions is a division of Houghton Mifflin Harcourt.

MATH SOLUTIONS® and associated logos are trademarks or registered trademarks of
Houghton Mifflin Harcourt Publishing Company. Other company names, brand names,
and product names are the property and/or trademarks of their respective owners.

*Executive Editor:* Jamie Ann Cross
*Developmental Editor:* Joanna Davis-Swing
*Production Manager:* Denise A. Botelho
*Cover design:* Vicki Tagliatela, Dandilion Designs
*Cover photos:* Veer, a Division of Corbis Corporation / iStockphoto LP
*Interior design and composition:* Denise Hoffman
*Interior images:* Pampa Independent School District, Texas
*Videographer:* Friday's Films, www.fridaysfilms.com

Printed in the United States of America.
2  3  4  5  6  7  8  9    0014    24  23  22  21  20  19  18  17
4510003684                          ABCDE

# A Message from Math Solutions

We at Math Solutions believe that teaching math well calls for increasing our understanding of the math we teach, seeking deeper insights into how students learn mathematics, and refining our lessons to best promote students' learning.

Math Solutions shares classroom-tested lessons and teaching expertise from our faculty of professional development consultants as well as from other respected math educators. Our publications are part of the nationwide effort we've made since 1984 that now includes

- more than five hundred face-to-face professional development programs each year for teachers and administrators in districts across the country;
- professional development books that span all math topics taught in kindergarten through high school;
- videos for teachers and for parents that show math lessons taught in actual classrooms;
- on-site visits to schools to help refine teaching strategies and assess student learning; and
- free online support, including grade-level lessons, book reviews, inservice information, and district feedback, all in our Math Solutions Online Newsletter.

For information about all of the products and services we have available, please visit our website at *www.mathsolutions.com.* You can also contact us to discuss math professional development needs by calling (800) 868-9092 or by sending an email to *info@mathsolutions.com.*

We're always eager for your feedback and interested in learning about your particular needs. We look forward to hearing from you.

# Contents

## Contents

## Chapter 3    Shared Classroom Experience    130

### Tools You Can Use

## Chapter 4    Mathematics Vertical Learning Team    166

# Contents

# List of Reproducibles

*The following reproducibles are referenced and used with individual collaboration structures.*

## List of Reproducibles

*All reproducibles are also available as downloadable, printable versions at www.mathsolutions.com/givemefivereproducibles.*

# Acknowledgments

Our gratitude and appreciation goes to all the educators in the Pampa Independent School District community who opened their hearts and minds to learn collaboratively in order to create powerful mathematics classrooms for their students. You are just amazing! A BIG thanks to Shirley Hord, who opened the door that allowed mathematics professional learning to manifest and that resulted in change and improvement.

# How to Use This Resource

 **Video Clip**

### Introduction

As you watch the video clip labeled "Introduction," consider the following questions:

- What do you think is happening?
- Can you identify some of the collaborative structures in action?
- Are they similar to what happens in your school? Why or why not?
- What are you interested in learning from this resource?

 The view this video clip, scan the QR code or access via mathsolutions.com/ GMFintro

## Why This Resource?

This resource provides the guidance and tools necessary to implement five coach–teacher–principal collaborations that have improved mathematics instruction for hundreds of students. The video clips and interviews invite you inside schools for a *seeing-is-believing* look at math coaches, teachers, and principals collaborating in action. Through these collaborations, schools in Pampa Independent School District, a Title 1 District (the majority of students come from low-income backgrounds), experienced significant, sustainable gains in student achievement. But, the increase isn't just in test scores; the environment of these schools has transformed profoundly. Travis Elementary principal Jill Faubion perhaps states it best, saying, "I have never seen so much excitement among my teachers about teaching math."

We like to say, "Give me five!"

> For more on the demographics of Pampa Independent School District, see Video Clip C.1: From the Administrator's Perspective.

**It Really Can Happen . . . Insights from the Field**

In just one year of experiencing the *Give Me Five!* collaboration process, Pampa Independent School District experienced significant, sustainable gains in student achievement. On end-of-year local math assessments, Wilson Elementary saw an increase in first-grade scores from 61 percent to 89 percent. In state assessments, Travis Elementary saw an increase in fourth-grade scores from 70 percent to 91 percent, and Lamar Elementary saw an increase in scores from 75 percent to 82 percent.

In our many years in education, we have seen a lot of people and programs come and go; but, throughout these changes we see one consistent correlation: the greatest impact on student learning is a result of daily collaboration among professional staff. How does a school create this daily collaboration? We found the secret to success resides in five simple, highly effective structures—and we are excited to share them.

## Do I Have Time for This?

In the day-to-day stresses of working in a school, it can feel like everyone is moving at a human speed equivalent to 100 miles per hour. Typically, from the first day of school to the last, teachers, principals, math coaches, and teacher leaders get caught up in independent waves of "doing." Consider the following statements. Have you heard them before?

"There's just no time to cover everything!"

"I'm always trying to play catch-up."

"We have to get through this before the test."

The collaborations in the *Give Me Five!* process are created to coexist with a school day, not add to it. When implemented correctly, they happen within and as close to the classroom as possible, and actually become a significant means to saving time and alleviating stress. The five collaborations provide a predictable, consistent space for teachers, principals, math coaches, and teacher leaders to come together with the intended and common purpose of deepening understanding about how to support student learning effectively.

# What Are the Five Collaborations? (An Overview)

Together, the five collaborations unite to form a learning system that can fuel professional learning for instructional improvement resulting in increased student achievement. From creating a shared vision and specific goals in the Strategic Planning Session to fostering professional learning in the three options for Professional Learning Communities to maintaining communication with an easy-to-implement management structure, the five collaborations provide a framework schools can implement to make a difference in math achievement. The heart of these collaborations is a focus on identifying student strategies for learning math, building teacher knowledge about underlying math concepts, designing and implementing lessons, assessing student understanding, and redesigning lessons to strengthen student support. A brief overview of each of the structures follows.

## Professional Learning Communities: Communities with a Purpose

Most schools set aside regular time for professional learning, often in the form of Professional Learning Communities. A problem we've seen with Professional Learning Communities is that all too often they lack a specific focus and devolve into chat sessions related only tangentially to mathematics learning. *Give Me Five!* offers three different types of Professional Learning Communities, each with a particular focus: the Mathematics Content Learning Team (Chapter 2), the Shared Classroom Experience (Chapter 3), and the Mathematics Vertical Learning Team (Chapter 4). We encourage schools and coaches to view these three structures as a menu of professional learning community options and to plug in the ones that best fit the needs of teachers and students in a particular school.

*"It's all about the teachers continuing their learning to make sure that they are meeting the needs of their students; it's a collaborative process of putting together good structures and strategies and understanding the math behind the math. And I think the most powerful thing is getting those collaborative structures in place."*

—Evan Smith, deputy superintendent

## Structure 1:  Strategic Planning Sessions

The first of the five structures, Strategic Planning Sessions are fundamental to getting teachers, math coaches, teacher leaders, and principals on the same page, sharing the same mindsets, commitments, actions, and behaviors that increase student achievement in mathematics. These sessions provide a time to define a vision, goals, and a plan of action to achieve goals—one, three, and five years from the present. Outcomes include educators imagining and articulating changes, identifying areas to strengthen, and naming actions to realize the changes. The Strategic Planning Sessions (typically, three are held each school year) are especially helpful in a changing environment, such as shifting to the Common Core State Standards for Mathematics and the increasing expectations of state standards.

## Structure 2:   Mathematics Content Learning Team

With this structure, grade-level teachers come together with math coaches and other teacher leaders to discuss and learn more about the math content at their grade level. This is a space to identify objectives and share effective instructional strategies.

## Structure 3:  Shared Classroom Experience

During a Shared Classroom Experience, professionals at different levels of the school system come together to team-teach—to share a classroom. The experience has four parts: (1) designing the lesson, (2) sharing the lesson with other participants, (3) teaching the lesson, and (4) reflecting on the lesson. We focus on two types of shared classroom experience: one in which two teachers come together to teach (peer teaching) and one in which a math coach and teacher come together to teach (unlike some coaching models in which the coach observes the teacher teaching, then gives feedback, this is a shared experience). In both scenarios, principals and other teacher leaders may be involved as active participants.

## Structure 4:   Mathematics Vertical Learning Team

Also referred to as vertical learning, during these meetings teachers across grade levels come together with math coaches and teacher leaders to understand how mathematics is taught at each grade level. By learning how standards are taught at each grade level, teachers are more equipped to recognize and work with students who are behind or ahead in the learning of a specific standard. This is also a space for teachers to share effective instructional strategies that can be adapted to various grade levels.

## Structure 5:   Ten-Minute Meeting

Last but not least, the Ten-Minute Meeting is a structured event that occurs when two or more school-based professionals, such as a math coach and principal, convene for ten minutes to reach agreement and share the same understanding of a key issue. It is a time to sit down face-to-face, in person or via technology (such as a conference call), and create the same language and responses to three key questions. In a climate of "there's no time to meet," this structure makes meeting not only doable, but highly efficient and effective.

**Your Turn**  **What Is Your School's Current Readiness for Learning?**

Think of your school system and consider these questions:

- What structures are currently in place on your campus to support ongoing professional learning?
- What do teachers talk about when they are together?
- Is time together a meeting or a learning experience?
- How do teachers interact with principals, teacher leaders, and math coaches? What do they share, related to student learning?
- What does a classroom in your school look like and sound like on a daily basis?
- How does your school culture support professional learning?

# Where and How Do I Begin?

We like to consider the design of this resource influenced by the "choose your own adventure" novels you might remember reading as a child. There are several directions you may choose in accessing the content—primarily, through two key entry points: the quick reference questions (Part I) or the five structures (Part II).

## Quick Reference Questions (Part I)

Part I is created to guide you through the content based on your role (math coach, teacher leader, teacher, or principal) and the key questions you might have. Are you a teacher? You may choose to start with the section "Quick Reference Questions for Teachers." You'll find a series of commonly asked questions focused on concerns encountered frequently by teachers. Find the question relevant to your need, and the answer will guide you to one or more of the five collaborations/structures that meet your needs most directly.

## The Five Collaboration Structures (Part II)

Alternatively, you may choose to dive right into the structures; we recommend this! The structures are presented in the order of implementation. Chapters 2 and 4 (Mathematics Content Learning Team and Mathematics Vertical Learning Team, respectively) are interchangeable. Each structure features video clips of the collaboration in action in an actual school, then explores the collaboration through friendly, multistep guides, Reproducibles, tips, and explanations. We've included everything you need to get started. At the end of every structure's presentation, there is a "Your Turn" element, which gives you the time-saving tools necessary for designing and implementing the collaboration—and prompt you to get started.

# Let Us Know What Works for You!

We encourage dialogue with you as you implement the five structures (after all, learning from each other is the heart of collaboration!). Whether you want to give or take five, please feel free to contact us at info@mathsolutions.com.

# Video Clip References

## Educators Starring in Video Clips

The following educators in the Pampa Independent School District community are featured in action in the Part II video clips; thank you for opening your doors.

| Strategic Planning Sessions | Video Clip 1.1 |
|---|---|
| Janice Bradley, author and facilitator | |
| Dana Cargill, author | |
| Evan Smith, deputy superintendent | |
| Jan Cleek, principal, Lamar Elementary | |
| Melissa True, principal, Wilson Elementary | |
| Beverly Underwood, principal, Austin Elementary | |
| Jill Faubion, principal, Travis Elementary | |
| Bree Reid, math coach, Wilson Elementary | |
| Andrea Wyatt, math coach, Austin Elementary | |
| Courtney Blackmon, math coach, Travis Elementary | |
| Jan Cory, math coach, Lamar Elementary | |
| Misty Hood, fourth-grade teacher, Austin Elementary | |
| Michelle Crowell, third-grade teacher, Wilson Elementary | |
| Tatiana Greer, second-grade teacher, Lamar Elementary | |

| Mathematics Content Learning Team | Video Clips 2.1, 2.2 |
|---|---|
| Janice Bradley, facilitator | |
| Jan Cleek, principal, Lamar Elementary | |
| Jan Cory, math coach, Lamar Elementary | |
| Laurie Lance, first-grade teacher, Lamar Elementary | |
| Tatiana Greer, second-grade teacher, Lamar Elementary | |

*(continued)*

# Video Clip References

# How to Access Online Video Clips

Readers have several options for accessing the video clips. Either scan the QR code (with a QR code reader app of your choice) that appears within the video clip section in the text or enter the corresponding URLs in your browser. If you would like to access all the clips at once, follow these instructions:

1. Go to mathsolutions.com/myvideos and click or tap the Create New Account button at the bottom of the Log In form.

2. Create an account, even if you have created one with Math Solutions bookstore. You will receive a confirmation email when your account has been created.

3. Once your account has been created, you will be taken to the Product Registration page. Click Register on the product you would like to access (in this case, *Give Me Five!*).

4. Enter key code **GMF5** and click or tap the Submit Key Code button.

5. Click or tap the Complete Registration button.

6. To access videos at any time, visit your account page.

Key Code:
**GMF5**

# Guidelines for Watching Videos

The teachers, coaches, and principals who agreed to be recorded in these videos have complex and challenging responsibilities, just like you. When we watch videos of others it is easy to see things that we might do differently. It is then all too easy to move to a critical stance, focusing on what "should" have been done differently. But we have found that such a stance is not helpful for learning.

These videos are not scripted or rehearsed. They are real sessions. Remember that teaching is a complicated activity, in which the teacher is required to do many things at once. As you watch these videos, alone or with others, we recommend following these rules:

1. Assume that there are many things you don't know about the students, the classroom, the school, and the shared history of everyone in the video.

2. Assume good intent and expertise on the part of the teacher, coach, and/or principal. If you cannot understand his or her actions, try to hypothesize what might have motivated him or her.

3. Keep focused on your observations about what everyone is getting out of the collaboration.

4. Keep focused on how the collaboration is serving the mathematical goals.

*Source:* Adapted from *Talk Moves: A Teacher's Guide for Using Talk Moves to Support the Common Core and More, Third Edition* by Suzanne H. Chapin, Catherine O'Connor, and Nancy Canavan Anderson (Math Solutions, 2013, xxi).

# Video Clips by Chapter

# Video Clips by Grade

| Video Clip Number and Title | Grade Level | | | | | |
|---|---|---|---|---|---|---|
| | K | 1 | 2 | 3 | 4 | 5 |
| Introduction | | | | | | |
| Video Clip A.1:  From the Math Coach's Perspective | | | | | | |
| Video Clip B.1:  From the Teacher's Perspective | | | | | | |
| Video Clip C.1:  From the Administrator's Perspective | | | | | | |
| Video Clip 1.1:  A Strategic Planning Session in Action | | | | | | |
| Video Clip 2.1:  A Mathematics Content Learning Team in Action | | • | • | | | |
| Video Clip 2.2:  Building Knowledge in a Mathematics Content Learning Team | | • | • | | | |
| Video Clip 3.1:  A Shared Classroom Experience: Briefing Observers | | • | • | | | |
| Video Clip 3.2:  A Shared Classroom Experience: Teaching the Lesson | | • | • | | | |
| Video Clip 3.3:  A Shared Classroom Experience: Reflecting on the Lesson | | • | • | | | |
| Video Clip 3.4:  A Shared Classroom Experience in Action | | | | | • | • |
| Video Clip 3.5:  The Power of a Shared Classroom Experience | • | | | | | |
| Video Clip 4.1:  A Mathematics Vertical Learning Team in Action | • | • | • | • | • | • |
| Video Clip 4.2:  Building Knowledge in a Mathematics Vertical Learning Team | • | • | • | • | • | • |
| Video Clip 5.1:  A Ten-Minute Meeting in Action | | | | | | |
| Video Clip 5.2:  Developing a Vision in a Ten-Minute Meeting | | | | | | |

# Quick Reference Questions

Research studies and our own experience have shown that when collaboration structures focused on professional learning are in place, coaches, teachers, and school administrators have the infrastructure they need to tackle almost any issue or problem that arises. That's the impetus behind this book—to present five structures that can be used flexibly to address almost any situation. All the information and tools needed to implement each structure are included in Part II of this book; but, before digging into the nuts and bolts of each one, it's helpful to see how they can be used to meet a variety of needs. In Part I, we present questions we hear over and over again at the schools with which we work. The questions are divided into three sections—questions from coaches and/or teacher leaders, from teachers, and from principals—and the answers demonstrate how to orchestrate the five structures to generate solutions that work for your particular situation. We also share helpful tips and resources that can support you in your journey toward mathematics success.

> "If the principal is not encouraging, supporting, and leading the school in the translation of the vision's ideas into day-to-day practice, the school will drift, its teachers will lose their focus, and students and parents will be denied the excitement of an education whose details are designed to offer them both discernment and meaning."
>
> —Seymour Fox

## Overview

# Quick Reference Questions for Coaches/Teacher Leaders

In this section, we present questions we typically hear from coaches as they work in schools supporting teachers and students to improve mathematics achievement. In the pages that follow, we examine how the five collaboration structures—the Strategic Planning Sessions, the Mathematics Content Learning Team, the Shared Classroom Experience, the Mathematics Vertical Learning Team, and the Ten-Minute Meeting—can be called on to help coaches and teacher leaders address a variety of challenges effectively.

## Overview

> Videos can be streamed by registering this product at mathsolutions.com/myvideos. See page xxiii for instructions.

## Tools You Can Use

> Tools You Can Use appear at the end of this section and are also available online at mathsolutions.com/givemefivereproducibles.

**Video Clip A.1**

### From the Math Coach's Perspective

*"Often at the elementary level, teachers are uncomfortable with math content. What we've found is that by providing them time to use resources, to plan together, and to check for understanding as far as the content knowledge goes, we're seeing sustainability among all the teachers—the collaboration, the professional learning communities; teachers are sharing their content knowledge. And it's been really valuable because they come to me and they say, 'I've never been comfortable teaching math, but now it's so fun.'"*

—Courtney Blackmon, math coach

To view this video clip, scan the QR code or access via mathsolutions.com/GMFA1

As you watch this clip, consider the following questions:

- In what ways can you relate to what this coach is feeling, thinking, or saying?
- What questions might you have as a coach?

**Question 1**    ## How do I get a clear description of my coach role? ...........

As one coach stated, "I need to know if the principal sees my role as a way to make mathematics education at our school more effective by working with teachers, or if I am just there to tutor struggling students and to accept other duties as assigned, such as being an assessment coordinator."

If this concern resonates with you, use the collaboration structures listed here to obtain clarity about your role as a coach or teacher leader.

**Strategic Planning Sessions** (see Chapter 1)

*How this structure helps address the question:*

- Gives the school a targeted focus for improving mathematics instruction
- Allows coaches, teachers, and principals to share the same vision and language of "coaching" and its implementation

- Allows coach to share ideas for working most effectively with teachers during the year to change educator practice
- Clarifies the roles and responsibilities of the coach

*(continued)*

**Ten-Minute Meeting** (see Chapter 5)

*How this structure helps address the question:*

- Allows the coach to clarify the coaching role with the principal and/or other teachers
- Enables the coach to build relational capacity with the principal and other teachers, and maintain communication

- Provides an opportunity for the coach to share ways of supporting a teacher, such as gathering resources, planning a lesson, or collecting data by listening to students' thinking, reasoning, and problem-solving strategies

**Question 2**    **How do the teachers understand my role as a coach?**

One coach shared this story: "I hear teachers talking about how they have searched for resources. I had those resources at my fingertips, but they did not ask me. They don't seem to understand I am here to support them in many ways. I can plan lessons, model lessons, give feedback, and solve problems regarding challenging students and difficult concepts. Also, some teachers don't want me in their classroom."

If this concern resonates with you, use the structures listed to here to help disseminate information about your role as a coach.

**Strategic Planning Sessions** (see Chapter 1)

*How this structure helps address the question:*

- Gives the coach the opportunity to collaborate with teachers to create a shared vision for mathematics instruction and professional learning
- Offers teachers a voice in shaping the coach's role as a math resource
- Allows the coach, the teachers, and the principal the opportunity to agree on the purpose of "coaching" and its implementation
- Offers the coach a chance to show teachers you are a learning partner, an educator committed to professional learning to serve students better
- Clarifies your role as a coach

**Ten-Minute Meeting** (see Chapter 5)

*How this structure helps address the question:*

- Provides an opportunity for the coach to collaborate with the principal and/or teachers about ways to develop a shared vision and purpose for "coaching" as part of an overall support system for student learning. When this vision is established, it can be communicated simply by including a note in an email to the staff, reminding them that student learning is the focus of the coaching role

**Question 3**   How do I get principals to support .................................
                 my coaching role?

One coach faced this situation: "The principal doesn't appear to be supportive of the learning teams or the Shared Classroom Experience. The teachers don't treat these times as valuable because the principal does not treat them as such—meaning, meetings are scheduled, but aren't taken seriously by teachers or attended by the principal."

If this concern resonates with you, use the structures listed here to build a relationship with your principal and collaborate to establish a shared vision of coaching at your school.

**Strategic Planning Sessions** (see Chapter 1)

*How this structure helps address the question:*

- Gives principals a clear picture of how their coaches and teachers envision math instruction
- Creates an Action Plan that shows clearly how professional learning teams and experiences will support changing teacher practices to effect student achievement
- Provides an opportunity for teachers and coaches to ask for support from the administration
- Clarifies the role of the coach with the principal and teachers in supporting math instruction and teacher learning
- Schedules team meetings and Shared Classroom Experience on the school calendar and protects those times as valuable

**Ten-Minute Meeting** (see Chapter 5)

*How this structure helps address the question:*

- Provides a time for the coach to talk with the principal about concerns and to clarify how the principal can support the coaching role and bolster coaching efforts
- Allows the principal and coach to share ideas together for how a coach can support teachers' professional learning, resulting in changing practices inside the classroom

5

**How do I work with teachers who are resistant to change?**

One coach reports: "Teachers view me as an evaluator and will not talk honestly to me. They are nervous to talk openly and seem on edge anytime I am in their classroom. Some teachers openly avoid eye contact with me or turn and walk the other way when they see me in the hallway."

If this coach's concern resonates with you, start with the Shared Classroom Experience structure detailed here. In your interactions with resistant teachers, be sure to do the following:

- Listen to the teacher's concerns first, before offering advice or suggestions.
- Offer support and ideas, but always keep in mind the classroom teacher knows the students.
- Find common ground. Focus conversations on what both of you can do to support student growth and improvement.
- Suggest ideas for next steps based on observations of student behaviors and work.
- Acknowledge and do not discount the teacher's experience. Teachers need to feel they still have power and ownership in what happens in their classroom.
- Avoid trying to "fix" the teacher. Keep your focus on supporting student learning and teaching that can improve student performance.
- Take it slow. If "baby steps" are taken, then teachers feel more secure about taking risks.
- Ask questions in a nonthreatening way to understand teachers' thinking. This will go a long way in understanding how to communicate and work with them.
- Make sure the teacher is successful and is never embarrassed in front of anyone observing the lesson. You are a learning partner and serve as a safety net.

**Shared Classroom Experience** (see Chapter 3)

*How this structure helps address the question:*

- Provides the coach and teacher an opportunity to collaborate on lesson planning, delivery, and assessment in a way that respects the teachers' role as an expert on their students' strengths and needs

- Allows the coach to participate as a co-teacher in a lesson, so the teacher sees the coach as a peer working toward the same goal

- Offers time for the teacher and coach to share observations and ideas for responding to student needs in a collaborative, nonthreatening setting

- Helps build a relationship between the coach and the teacher

**Ten-Minute Meeting** (see Chapter 5)

*How this structure helps address the question:*

- Provides a time for the coach and the teachers to "get on the same page" with three questions that are important to both of you, such as: What can we learn to do together to increase students' understanding of place-value concepts?

- Allows for a concentrated time to listen to teachers' point of view and perspective to understand more fully their concerns and needs

- Allows the coach and teachers to share ideas for how to intervene with diverse populations, with students who are struggling to master math standards, and/or with students who need extensions

**Question 5**     **How do I work at different schools? How can I differentiate effectively the needs of teachers when I have to work at different schools?**

Consider this coach's situation: "I work at several different schools, and each principal and the teachers have a different idea of my role as a math coach."

    If this concern resonates with you, use the collaboration structures listed here to support your work at multiple schools. As a practical matter, we find it helpful to maintain a binder with a section for each school where you can keep copies of key documents from each school (such as the Action Plan) as well as notes from meetings at each campus. In addition, we recommend you capitalize on any technology available that allows you to participate in meetings remotely. Many districts have their own way to create webinars and interactive seminars, so ask your technology department to help you set up conferencing. Note that this type of collaboration is generally more successful if teachers have met each other in person first.

**Strategic Planning Sessions** (see Chapter 1)

*How this structure helps address the question:*

- Allows the coach to see each school's vision and Action Plan—its road map for improving mathematics instruction

- Clarifies the role each school expects the coach to play

- Helps coaches identify the specific needs at each school

*(continued)*

### Mathematics Content
**Learning Team** (see Chapter 2)

*How this structure helps address the question:*

- Allows the coach to support each school's specific math needs based on student data and teacher needs.

- Enables the coach to address the professional learning needs of teachers and identify subsequent contextual interventions needed by the specific populations of students. Not only do the populations and needs of students differ from school to school, but also the professional learning needs of teachers differ as well. For example, one school's data may show that developing fraction concepts is needed at fourth-grade level, but another school's fourth-grade data indicate fraction operations are in need of development.

### Mathematics Vertical
**Learning Team** (see Chapter 4)

*How this structure helps address the question:*

- Allows the coach to respond to the specific professional learning needs of teachers and to identify interventions for students

- Enables the coach to develop a broader view of the specific needs of a school's math program. Where are the gaps across the grade levels? What are the curriculum, instruction, and assessment needs?

"We've become more collaborative and that's not only collaborative within our departments, but it's also collaborative with the students. It's become a much more comfortable sharing of our talents. Whether we're on the giving end or the receiving end, we've learned that we can learn from everybody."

—Barry Haenisch, superintendent

## Question 6    How do I know if I'm making an impact?

One coach expressed this concern: "I work with teachers and students in and out of the classroom, but some days I don't feel as though I am helping anyone. At the end of the year, I'm not sure if I have been successful."

If this concern resonates with you, use the Shared Classroom Experience collaboration structure listed here to assess whether the professional learning experiences and coaching you provide are making a difference in teacher practice.

### Shared Classroom Experience (see Chapter 3)

*How this structure helps address the question:*

- Provides a powerful opportunity to hear what the teachers are thinking during the planning stage; for instance, the coach can observe whether teachers are taking more risks and listening and supporting each other actively

- Provides a chance to observe teachers' practices inside the classroom and to determine whether teachers reflect the professional learning outside the classroom

- Gives the coach the opportunity to observe teacher talk in the classroom, noticing, for instance, if the teacher is focusing on deepening student learning or just "covering" a topic

- Allows the coach to observe whether teachers are using misconceptions or wrong answers as opportunities to discover what a student is thinking

- Enables the coach to determine whether the teacher is able to discern which students are confused or don't "get it," as opposed to noticing who got the right answer

- Offers a chance to reflect on the experience: Was the teacher focused on what the students were learning? What were his or her actions?

### Ten-Minute Meeting (see Chapter 5)

*How this structure helps address the question:*

- Provides a time for the coach and teachers to discuss the changes the teachers made to classroom practice. If you schedule a Ten-Minute Meeting with grade levels, or with specific individuals two to three times during the year, you can track the changes teachers make to practice. For example, if a teacher says she increased her use of questioning at greater levels of rigor, and you observe this in the classroom, then you will know your focus and conversations on effective questioning had positive results.

9

**Question 7**   **How do I communicate effectively with principals?**

One coach shared this situation: "I never see my principal. She is so busy that, when I *can* catch her, we always get interrupted by something else that needs her immediate attention."

If this concern resonates with you, use the Ten-Minute Meeting to schedule purposeful discussions of key issues.

**Ten-Minute Meeting** (see Chapter 5)

*How this structure helps address the question:*

- Offers a manageable time commitment for even the busiest principal

- Focuses the principal's attention on one or two key goals at a time; helps to prioritize in case one goal only can be addressed in the time allotted

- Provides privacy and focus to obtain the principal's input on how the coach can best make a difference in supporting change related to the school's vision and Action Plan

- Creates a time to develop shared understanding and language about key issues at the school

**Question 8**   **What kind of feedback is most effective for improving teaching and learning?**

A coach shared this statement: "On a recent school survey, more than half the teachers said they wanted more feedback from me. I'm not sure what kind of feedback they want, or how to give it in a way that teachers will receive it positively."

If this concern resonates with you, all five structures provide opportunities to identify more clearly the role of feedback and the types of feedback that would improve teaching and students' mathematical understanding.

**Strategic Planning Sessions** (see Chapter 1)

*How this structure helps address the question:*

- Allows the coach to see each school's vision and the actions to take, which will inform the type of feedback necessary for improving mathematics instruction

- Clarifies the role each school expects from the coach and the type of feedback that will be received constructively

- Helps the coach identify the specific needs at each school, and the type of feedback needed for changes in math instruction

**Mathematics Content Learning Team** (see Chapter 2)

*How this structure helps address the question:*

- Allows the coach to identify the types of content-focused feedback needed for improving student learning
- Clarifies the role of feedback needed in a particular content area, such as how to shift students' additive thinking to multiplicative thinking

**Shared Classroom Experience** (see Chapter 3)

*How this structure helps address the question:*

- Allows the coach to assess the type of feedback useful to teachers' growth, and to practice both giving and receiving feedback in a structured context
- Creates a place to share feedback with teachers and the principal, and to assess results

**Mathematics Vertical Learning Team** (see Chapter 4)

*How this structure helps address the question:*

- Allows the coach to identify feedback needed across the grade levels, such as helping students to show, describe, and demonstrate their mathematical representations
- Clarifies the type of feedback needed to change instruction across grade levels

**Ten-Minute Meeting** (see Chapter 5)

*How this structure helps address the question:*

- Creates time for the coach and teachers to discuss the role of feedback as a means for change and improvement
- Clarifies the type of feedback that will push teachers' thinking and growth
- Helps the coach reflect on the outcomes of feedback from the teacher's point of view. How has the feedback provided by the teachers been meaningful? How could feedback improve?

**What kind of coaching support is available for my professional growth?**

One coach expressed, "This is my first year as a coach. Last year, I was a fourth-grade teacher here at the same school. Each month I attend meetings, spread out over eight to ten days, away from my school site, but the meetings aren't helping me with my day-to-day coaching. They are more management, curriculum, and data meetings. Where can I get support to learn how to coach teachers better?"

If this concern resonates with you, try a Ten-Minute Meeting with a person of influence, such as a principal or coaching supervisor, who can provide opportunities for growth and support for your coaching role.

**Ten-Minute Meeting** (see Chapter 5)

*How this structure helps address the question:*

- Clarifies expectations of the coaching role with the principal or supervisor
- Offers a chance to discuss the type of support needed to realize changes in educator practices
- Provides the opportunity to share needs and concerns for professional learning growth

**What can I do to reestablish a coaching relationship with teachers when it gets off to a rough start?**

One coach remarked, "Last year, I had some challenges building relationships with several of the teachers. They resented me coming into their room and were resistant to coaching. This year, I am expected to be in their classrooms more and to provide more support and feedback. It's uncomfortable, and I'm not sure what to do to fix things."

If this concern resonates with you, try a Ten-Minute Meeting with individuals and/or grade-level teams to reset the relationship. Participate in either or both the Mathematics Content Learning Team and the Mathematics Vertical Learning Team to show your interest and support for student learning, along with your willingness to provide support for teachers as they advance student learning.

**Mathematics Content Learning Team** (see Chapter 2)

*How this structure helps address the question:*

- Allows the coach to be seen as a listener and supporter of the school's vision for improved student learning
- Clarifies the role each team expects the coach to play in advancing students' math knowledge and skills at a specific grade level

## Mathematics Vertical Learning Team (see Chapter 4)

*How this structure helps address the question:*

- Allows the coach be seen as a listener and supporter of the school's vision for improved student learning
- Clarifies the role each team expects the coach to play in advancing students' math knowledge and skills across the grade levels

## Ten-Minute Meeting (see Chapter 5)

*How this structure helps address the question:*

- Provides time for the coach to listen to teachers' needs and to understand better their point of view related to their past experiences with coaching
- Clarifies the role of both teacher and coach in the coaching relationship
- Helps the coach reestablish and redefine the purpose of coaching

*"Coaches, teachers, principals—we come together throughout our district to share a vision and common goal: to help students feel successful and comfortable in the classroom environment, talk about math, speak up, and hold a math conversation."*

—Meagan Little Rankin, second-grade teacher

## Ten Tips for Coaching within a Culture of Professional Growth and Collaboration

In your work supporting teachers and students to strengthen mathematics achievement, keep the following tips in mind.

1.  **Build relational capacity first.**  Relational capacity is the level of trust and safety among educators in a school system, such as between a coach and a teacher. The degree of influence a coach has on a teacher is related directly to the relational capacity. The coach's opinions, beliefs, and guidance are more influential if the teacher feels safe with, not threatened by, the coach (Bryk and Schneider 2003). Be transparent when building and maintaining trust by sharing information, needs, and concerns in honest, open ways.

2.  **Focus on instruction that impacts student learning, not on the teacher's actions.**  Keep the conversation focused on students first—on the impact of instruction on student learning. Refrain from using the personal pronouns *you* or *I*. Instead of asking: What can *you* do differently? Ask: What can be done differently? It is a less threatening manner of speaking and won't put teachers on the defensive.

3.  **Recognize that opening up classrooms is a big risk for many teachers.**  Opening doors and sharing classroom practice can be scary. Teachers' anxiety results from the fact that their work and behaviors are being judged during classroom walkthroughs, teacher evaluations, and student performance. Having your performance and behavior scrutinized constantly creates pressures, which can result in anxiety for anyone—especially teachers. Listen, first, to how teachers feel about sharing their classroom, then acknowledge openly that your intentions are not to judge or evaluate, but instead to learn alongside them to choose instruction intentionally that supports students.

4.  **Start slow. Focus on making one change at a time through SMART (specific, measurable, attainable, relevant, and timely) goals.**  To set a SMART goal, begin with the frame: I will [do what] [where] [how often] and [by when]. For example, a teacher's SMART goal might be: I will post math learning objectives in student-friendly language on the whiteboard each day for five days this week. A coach's SMART goal might be: I will engage in two cycles of co-planning and co-teaching with second- and fifth-grade teachers this week. Check on the goals each week to see how they were met and what was learned. Set a new SMART goal every week. Momentum will build as both teachers and the coach advance their practice and share their successes with each other.

5.  **Be outcomes and results focused.**  During coaching conversations, envision the end result, not the activity first. Often, coaching conversations between a coach and teacher are activity focused and not outcome focused. Instead of asking: What are you going to do differently? Ask: If explicit instruction is used to support the standard of fraction equivalency, what will change for students? Instead of asking: What resources do you need? Ask: If number puzzles are used, what approaches can be anticipated from students?

6.  **Identify the knowledge, skills, and experience that both coach and teacher bring to the coaching relationship.**  Building the coach–teacher relationship is essential for ensuring instructional improvement that results in increased student achievement. A solid starting point is creating partnership agreements that define the coach–teacher working relationship and expectations for each other's roles

(Killion et al. 2012). A helpful tool is to use a star with five points. Write *Student Learning* at the center to identify the coach and teacher's shared goal. The coach and teacher then work together to identify five strengths each brings to the coaching relationship and records them at the tips of the star points. The final product is a star with the ten unique strengths the coach and teacher bring to supporting student learning—two strengths per point—five for the coach and five for the teacher.

7. **Create quality feedback loops between coach and teachers, and teachers and coach.**
A feedback loop occurs when the coach provides teachers or learning team members feedback about either teacher or student behaviors that prompts them to take positive actions. The type of feedback you give can make or break whether teachers can act on your feedback for change and improvement. It's important to understand different types of feedback and when to give each type. Instead of saying: You could have done this [put students into groups] instead of this [asked them to work alone]. Instead, say: The lesson had a clear objective, five students had opportunities to share, and the summary tied learning back to the objective. In the next lesson, how can more students have opportunities to respond? Feedback types include diagnosing why something is not working, helping teachers understand what they should be doing differently, and describing performance and the nuances, tweaks, or minor adjustments that can be made to support instruction leading to improved student learning (Jackson 2008). Try creating a feedback loop that goes from teacher to coach, along with coach-to-teacher feedback.

8. **Take risks, such as modeling a lesson with teachers.** Taking a risk means you are willing to try something, even though you fear something unpleasant may happen. If you are a new elementary school coach who has only had middle school experience, you may feel anxious about modeling a kindergarten lesson. Be honest with the teachers and enlist their help and guidance. Don't feel that you have to perform and be perfect! You are creating a learning partnership through your coaching in which everyone gains new knowledge and skills. By putting yourself in risk-taking situations, such as modeling a lesson with an unfamiliar grade level, you are modeling risk-taking behaviors—a characteristic needed by teachers to try new strategies for changing practice.

9. **Listen to teachers to understand their point of view and assess their concerns, and paraphrase their words to indicate they are being listened to carefully.** Often, coaches can be so focused on giving teachers feedback to improve instruction they forget to listen to teachers' points of view.

10. **During the coach–teacher interaction, let the teacher begin the conversation half the time.**
Often in coach–teacher relationships, the coach starts every conversation. This positions the coach as "higher up" in the relationship. Half the time, teachers should begin the conversation with their reflections and thoughts, instead of the coach always beginning the conversation. Sometimes, a coach's questions, delivery style, and tone of voice can cause teachers to feel quizzed, judged, or evaluated, or supported professionally through inquiry and dialogue. The desired result is a professional dialogue—a reciprocal exchange of information between teacher and coach designed for both to consider thoughtfully more effective instruction to affect student learning.

# Helpful Resources
# for Coaches/Teacher Leaders

*The Math Coach Field Guide: Charting Your Course* edited by
Carolyn Felux and Paula Snowdy (2006)

This resource is organized into eleven chapters that provide glimpses into the
work of coaches. Each chapter includes a description of the lived experience
of a math coach who has dealt with a variety of challenges and issues when
implementing coaching. Coaches can use this resource to gain different
perspectives on coaching, to differentiate coaching based on differing
teacher needs and styles, and to create a shared language of coaching.

*Quality Teaching in a Culture of Coaching* by Stephen Barkley (2010)

*Quality Teaching in a Culture of Coaching* describes a school culture in which
each teacher is responsible for the growth of every student, and in which
educators work together with teachers to move the school beyond being a
"status quo school" toward being a highly effective school. This book, which
is organized into three broad sections, provides a framework for establishing
a culture of coaching in the educational environment.

*Content-Focused Coaching: Transforming Mathematics Lessons*
by Lucy West and Fritz C. Staub (2003)

This book describes a professional learning model designed to engage both
teachers and coaches in thoughtful dialogues resulting in improved math
teaching and student learning. The model of content-focused coaching
provides a collaborative partnership between math specialists and teachers
to plan, teach, and reflect on classroom lessons. Specialists differentiate
for content, process, and context to provide individualized, adaptive, and
situation-specific professional learning focused on content, pedagogy,
and student learning.

# Quick Reference Questions for Teachers

In this section, we present questions we typically hear from teachers as they work in schools committed to improving students' math achievement. We examine how the five collaboration structures—the Strategic Planning Session, the Mathematics Content Learning Team, the Shared Classroom Experience, the Mathematics Vertical Learning Team, and the Ten-Minute Meeting—can be called on to help teachers address a variety of challenges effectively.

## Overview

> Videos can be streamed by registering this product at mathsolutions.com/myvideos. See page xxiii for instructions.

## Tools You Can Use

> Tools You Can Use appear at the end of this section and are also available online at mathsolutions.com/givemefivereproducibles.

# Give Me Five!

## From the Teacher's Perspective

*I think that any teacher who has an opportunity to peer teach with another teacher should jump at that opportunity. The lesson that we taught today likely with one teacher would have normally taken two days. But because we were both in there and we had the support of our principal and our math coach, we were able to cover a lot more ground.*

—Laurie Lance, first-grade teacher

To view this video clip, scan the QR code or access via mathsolutions.com/GMFB1

As you watch this clip, consider the following questions:

- In what ways can you relate to what this teacher is feeling, thinking, or saying?
- What questions might you have as a teacher?

## Question 1 — What can I do if students are coming to my classroom without basic skills?

One teacher shared this concern: "My fifth-grade students don't know their basic facts and I don't have time to teach them with all the standards I have to address. We are now into finding common denominators with fractions, and the students don't know their factors and multiples. Help!"

If this teacher's problem resonates with you, use the collaboration structures listed here, both to prevent the problem from occurring in the future and to develop strategies to support students and bring them up to grade level.

### Strategic Planning Sessions (see Chapter 1)

*How this structure helps address the question:*

- Sets a vision for mathematics instruction that all teachers create
- Fosters a sense of shared responsibility for collective improvement in ensuring effective instruction occurs at every grade level so students do not leave unprepared for the next grade

### Mathematics Content Learning Team (see Chapter 2)

*How this structure helps address the question:*

- Develops teachers' understanding of mathematical content at their grade level
- Allows teachers time to share instructional strategies and differentiation tips
- Creates time to assess student work collaboratively to identify students' misconceptions and gaps, then choose the appropriate place to intervene

- Provides time for teachers to study math content standards and mathematical practices at their grade level to know where to intervene

**Shared Classroom Experience** (see Chapter 3)

*How this structure helps address the question:*

- Allows teachers to spend more time with students to discover their misconceptions and gaps in understanding
- Offers additional insight into students' performance from other educators who may hear students thinking from a different point of view
- Enables teachers to strategize instructional options with educators who are familiar with the challenges faced by students

**Mathematics Vertical Learning Team** (see Chapter 4)

*How this structure helps address the question:*

- Allows teachers to see the progression of skills from one grade to another, so they can identify prerequisite skills
- Provides teachers time to develop consistent vocabulary so students will not be confused by a change in vocabulary at each grade level
- Supports teachers' deepening of their math content knowledge to know how to support students' understanding during instruction
- Provides time for teachers to study math content standards and mathematical practices across the grade levels to know where to intervene

---

**Question 2** | **What are some ways to support emergent bilingual students in accessing mathematics?**

One teacher noted, "I know that language should not be a barrier to a student's understanding of a math concept, but sometimes when I work with students not proficient in English, they seem to understand math procedures, yet have difficulty with language-rich problem solving. So much of our state assessment is language based."

If this concern resonates with you, use the collaboration structures listed here to determine the best ways to support emergent bilingual students in your classroom.

**Shared Classroom Experience** (see Chapter 3)

*How this structure helps address the question:*

- Allows teachers to learn the vocabulary used in previous grades, so the same language can be used, providing consistency for emergent bilingual students

- Allows teachers to share resources so that if one grade level has something that might benefit another group of students, they can share—especially manipulatives, pictures, or any resource that would make a concept more accessible to emergent bilingual students

*(continued)*

- Gives teachers opportunities to learn and apply strategies for language development—speaking, listening, reading, writing—and to integrate these strategies into planning lessons, instruction, and assessment
- Provides an equity lens to determine how teachers allow emergent bilingual students to participate during the lesson to access worthwhile mathematics

**Mathematics Vertical Learning Team** (see Chapter 4)

*How this structure helps address the question:*

- Enables teachers across grades to share the language they use so math vocabulary is consistent for students from year to year
- Develops teachers' understanding of how concepts were taught previously, resulting in student learning, which provides a reference for teachers as concepts are expanded, and offers consistency for emergent bilingual students
- Provides teachers opportunities to learn how to incorporate language development strategies across the grades

---

**Question 3** — **How can students be assessed other than with a grade?**

One teacher asked, "How can I know a student really understands a concept and can use several approaches to each problem? Just using worksheets and written exams might not give me a true picture of a student's understanding of or misconceptions with the math standards."

If this concern resonates with you, use the collaboration structures listed here to explore alternatives for assessment.

**Mathematics Content Learning Team** (see Chapter 2)

*How this structure helps address the question:*

- Allows grade-level teams to share and develop a variety of common, formative, and end-of-unit assessments
- Enables teams to share the results of a variety of summative and formative assessments, and to understand how to use these results to inform instructional decision making

**Shared Classroom Experience** (see Chapter 3)

*How this structure helps address the question:*

- Offers multiple educators the opportunity to take anecdotal notes during a lesson, providing evidence of what students say or do that enables the classroom teacher to assess their mathematical knowledge

- Allows multiple educators to ask questions to further students' mathematical thinking

- Provides an opportunity to plan for and use formative assessment strategies, then observe results with students

**Mathematics Vertical Learning Team** (see Chapter 4)

*How this structure helps address the question:*

- Allows teachers across grade levels to understand the purpose of formative assessment and to share ideas for assessments

- Provides the opportunity for teachers at multiple grade levels to assess a student work sample to identify whether a student is working at, below, or above grade level

---

**Question 4** **How do I collaborate with my principal and math coach?**

As one teacher shared, "I am not sure my principal or math coach remembers what it is like to be in a classroom with students at all different levels of learning. My kids are losing out, and I want more feedback on what to do differently. Here it is in January and no one has been in my room this entire school year. The math coach is so busy with entering assessment data, and I don't see the principal."

If this concern resonates with you, use the collaboration structures listed here to build a relationship with your principal and math coach for successful collaboration.

**Shared Classroom Experience** (see Chapter 3)

*How this structure helps address the question:*

- Provides an opportunity to work closely with the math coach and the principal while planning a lesson

- Provides an opportunity for the students to see the principal and math coach in a teacher role, and shows clearly to the students that the math coach, teacher, and principal are collaborating to learn together

- Allows the principal to observe students and get to know them as learners

- Offers the chance for multiple educators to brainstorm ideas together that support their students' math growth

**Ten-Minute Meeting** (see Chapter 5)

*How this structure helps address the question:*

- Provides an opportunity for teachers to share a particular mathematical learning concern with the principal or math coach

- Allows time for educators to get on the same page with support—that is, to identify types of support needed for teachers to advance instruction for student learning

**What can I do if a principal supports traditional, behaviorist approaches to math teaching and I want to try more constructivist approaches?**

One teacher shared this situation: "My principal thinks that a quiet classroom is a learning classroom. In my classroom, the students are discussing and explaining their knowledge. When I get feedback from his learning walks, and on my formal evaluation, I get low ratings in the Learning Environment section."

If this concern resonates with you, use the collaboration structures listed here to express your ideas and begin to effect change.

### Strategic Planning Sessions (see Chapter 1)

*How this structure helps address the question:*

- Provides the opportunity to craft a common vision of mathematics instruction; all teachers have a voice and the group reaches consensus about the vision

- Provides an opportunity to clarify what one can expect to observe in an effective mathematics classroom

- Uses data, standards, and research-based best practices to inform discussion about a school or district's Vision Statement and Action Plan

### Ten-Minute Meeting (see Chapter 5)

*How this structure helps address the question:*

- Allows teachers to clarify how an approach supports a school's vision for mathematics instruction

- Gives teachers the opportunity to share professional learning with the principal and determine together whether to implement a new approach

- Provides an opportunity for a teacher to present a rationale for using different, research-based methods and to identify the types of support needed to bolster student learning

See the Helpful Resources for Administrators on page 48 for materials you can share with your principal.

*"I don't get nervous teaching math anymore. I can read through the lessons, talk to my math coach, talk with teachers from other grades, talk with my coworkers. I'm not afraid of it anymore and it makes sense."*

—Laurie Lance, first-grade teacher

## Question 6   How do I "cover" all the standards?

Consider this teacher's concern: "I'm not sure how to address all the state's math standards in one year. What can I do to teach everything?"

If this concern resonates with you, use the collaboration structures listed here to develop your knowledge of the mathematics content in your standards and to collaborate with other teachers about how best to address the required content that will result in student learning throughout the course of a school year.

### Mathematics Content
### Learning Team (see Chapter 2)

*How this structure helps address the question:*

- Allows teachers to deepen their mathematics content knowledge at their particular grade level and to identify priority standards for their grade level

- Offers a chance to develop a scope and sequence and pacing guide to ensure standards are addressed, not "covered" over the year

- Provides the opportunity to analyze students' work to determine their understandings and misconceptions

- Offers a time to create a collective educator mindset shift from "covering the content standards" to addressing and deepening the standards at the same grade level through student development of mathematical practices

### Shared Classroom Experience (see Chapter 3)

*How this structure helps address the question:*

- Allows teachers to understand jointly how a particular lesson engages students at high cognitive levels and supports students' development of state math standards—both content and mathematical practices

- Creates a time for changing educator mindsets, dispositions, and language about "learning," not "teaching to," the standards. The Shared Classroom Experience promotes a shift in thinking about students learning, not teachers teaching, the standards.

### Mathematics Vertical
### Learning Team (see Chapter 4)

*How this structure helps address the question:*

- Allows teachers to analyze how content articulates vertically across grade levels as identified in the state standards

- Helps teachers prioritize which standards need more time in particular grade levels

- Provides the opportunity to design lessons that address the standards in partnership with other teachers, then evaluate the effectiveness of the lessons and revise them to improve them

- Offers a time to create a collective educator mindset shift from "covering the content standards" to addressing and deepening the standards across the grade levels through  student development of mathematical practices

23

**What do I use to teach math? The textbook, the district** .................. **curriculum map, or the standards?**

One teacher shared this situation: "I'm so confused. I've been told by the district to follow the textbook with fidelity, use the district curriculum map, and teach to the state standards. I'm finding that many of my students are struggling as I rush to stay apace. I just discovered at a district training session that several textbook lessons don't align with the standards. I'm not sure what I'm supposed to pay attention to when I teach math."

If this concern resonates with you, use the collaboration structures listed here to develop your understanding of what lessons—designed using your state content standards and mathematical practices—look like and sound like.

### Mathematics Content Learning Team (see Chapter 2)

*How this structure helps address the question:*

- Allows teachers to deepen their math content knowledge of the standards for teaching at their particular grade level

- Gives teachers the opportunity to design lessons for students to learn and gain mastery of standards

- Provides time for teachers to "connect the dots" —to learn how to plan math units and lessons with their standards, curriculum map, and textbook

### Shared Classroom Experience (see Chapter 3)

*How this structure helps address the question:*

- Allows teachers, math coaches, and principals to understand jointly how a particular lesson can be planned to engage students at high cognitive levels while supporting all students' mastery of content standards and mathematical practices

- Gives teachers and math coaches time to plan a lesson together, and practice using their recommended resources

- Creates an opportunity for principals, teachers, and math coaches to develop a shared mindset—to "get on the same page"—about how to align the standards, textbook, and curriculum map, and use them effectively for promoting students' mathematical knowledge and skills

**Question 8**    **How do I find the time to collaborate?** .................................................

One teacher faced this situation: "The district has just told us that we need more time for collaboration. Where are we going to find time in our busy day to collaborate? I don't like collaboration. When our grade level gets together, we just waste a lot of time. Where do we find the time and what would make a good use of the time?"

If this concern resonates with you, use the structures listed here to find time for collaboration—and implement strategies to make that time productive.

**Shared Classroom Experience** (see Chapter 3)

*How this structure helps address the question:*

- Provides the opportunity and structure for teachers to plan lessons together, teach them together, then reflect on lesson implementation

- Gives teachers a planning process so they can create an effective lesson in a reasonable amount of time

- Provides an example of how to use collaboration time productively, which results in new knowledge, skills, and mindsets about math teaching and learning

**Ten-Minute Meeting** (see Chapter 5)

*How this structure helps address the question:*

- Allows teachers an opportunity to meet with the principal and math coach to explore ways to find time and create a clear purpose for collaborating for learning

- Clarifies issues that are preventing collaboration for learning—namely, how to use time most effectively within existing learning team structures, such as Mathematics Content Learning Team meetings. Often, structures for collaboration lack a focus for learning and guidance for conversations that result in a productive outcome.

- Provides time for exploring scheduling that will allow for additional time for teacher collaboration during the work day

For more on establishing norms on collaboration, see page 58.

**After looking at the data, what can I do differently** ............................. **and how can I do it?**

A teacher leader who is part of a turnaround school program remarked, "We have data meetings each week to analyze student data. The problem is that we don't have time to talk about what to do differently with the data findings. Last week, the data showed that the lowest scores in third grade were about representing problems using multiplication and division. I really don't know what to do differently with this information for scores to improve by next week."

If this concern resonates with you, use the collaboration structures listed here to learn new knowledge, skills, and strategies for changing practices to create improvement in student learning.

### Mathematics Content
**Learning Team** (see Chapter 2)

*How this structure helps address the question:*

- Allows teachers to deepen their math content knowledge of the standards at each grade level that students are not mastering
- Gives teachers the opportunity to learn new grouping and instructional strategies for improving student learning
- Provides time for teachers to learn how to plan math units and lessons, incorporating new strategies that support student needs as identified through data analysis

### Mathematics Vertical
**Learning Team** (see Chapter 4)

*How this structure helps address the question:*

- Allows teachers to deepen their math content knowledge of the standards that students are not mastering across grade levels
- Gives teachers the opportunity to learn new grouping and instructional strategies for improving student learning
- Provides time for teachers to make vertical connections for supporting student needs as identified through data analysis

### Shared Classroom Experience (see Chapter 3)

*How this structure helps address the question:*

- Provides the opportunity and structure for teachers to plan lessons together, incorporating strategies that support student needs as identified through data analysis
- Gives teachers, the math coach, and the principal an opportunity to link student needs (identified by the data) with actual strategies that support students, and to make those strategies visible

## Question 10  How do I increase student engagement during a math lesson?

A teacher shared the following comment: "I need help increasing student engagement during my math lessons. Feedback from the principal from her last formal evaluation was that student engagement was low. She said that she did not hear students talking about math enough of the time, and suggested I find some professional learning or resources that would give me strategies for increasing student engagement."

If this concern resonates with you, use the collaboration structures listed here to learn new knowledge, skills, and strategies for increasing student engagement during a math lesson.

### Mathematics Content Learning Team (see Chapter 2)

*How this structure helps address the question:*

- Allows teachers to address the kind of instructional strategies needed to engage students at a specific grade level in math content at a higher level of cognitive demand

- Gives teachers the opportunity to learn how to develop and increase student use of mathematical practices at a specific grade level

### Mathematics Vertical Learning Team (see Chapter 4)

*How this structure helps address the question:*

- Allows teachers to address the kind of instructional strategies needed to engage students across the grade levels in math content at a higher level of cognitive demand

- Gives teachers the opportunity to learn how to develop and increase student use of mathematical practices across the grade levels

### Shared Classroom Experience (see Chapter 3)

*How this structure helps address the question:*

- Provides the opportunity and structure for teachers to plan lessons together, integrating strategies to increase student engagement intentionally

- Creates an opportunity to enact the planned strategies for increasing student engagement during an actual math lesson

- Provides time for teachers, the math coach, and the principal to learn together about how to increase student engagement collectively

## Ten Tips for Teaching within a Culture of Professional Growth and Collaboration

1. **Know the outcomes—the purpose and expectations—for participation in one of the five collaboration structures.** Ask for clarification about what you are to learn and what you are to do when you meet. For example, by the end of the meeting, what do you want to have accomplished? What do you want to know more about personally? What does the team need to know?

2. **Come to the meeting with an open mind for learning and gaining new knowledge and skills.** Be ready to learn with a reflective disposition—that is, to examine successes and challenges with an eye toward improving opportunities for student learning. Learn and gain new knowledge from your own personal beliefs and experience, from knowledgeable others, and from research. Presume positive intentions from colleagues and be willing to explore ideas toward gaining new knowledge. Be willing to consider new ideas and skills, and learn whether these new strategies will result in changes and improvements to student learning.

3. **Develop and use norms for learning collaboration.** Often, norms are developed to manage behavior, but it is also powerful to adopt norms that offer guidelines for learning together productively. See the discussion on page 59 for more detail.

4. **Participate fully in every professional learning structure.** Add your ideas to the conversation to share your thinking with fellow teachers. All will benefit when open and honest communication occurs.

5. **Open your classroom to the Shared Classroom Experience.** The classroom is like a learning lab—a place to take risks and try new ideas in the safety of a collaborative experience. Everyone suspends evaluation and judgment during this time. The adults model collaborative learning for the students, and the students benefit from the shared knowledge of all educators in the room.

6. **Understand the math coach's role on your campus.** The math coach can be your best source of support for adopting instructional practices that increase student learning. The math coach's role is, ideally, to provide feedback, instructional strategies, and resources, and to serve as a learning partner for solving problems of practice. The math coach and you should be able to share your teaching practice together, resulting in new knowledge and skills for supporting students' math learning.

7. **Keep conversations focused on student learning, not on critiquing teaching.**
   Ask: What are students learning? What do they understand? Not understand? What strategies can be used to support our emergent bilingual students? Gifted students? As you consider these questions, consider options for teaching.

8. **Maintain an objective—not personal—focus on student learning.** One way to keep the discussion objective is to minimize the use of personal pronouns and focus on the topic, task, or solution. Ask: What strategies can be used to support place value understanding? Don't ask: What can you do differently?

9. **Move from speaking in generalizations to speaking as specifically as possible.**
   For example, instead of saying, "My kids can't multiply," say, "More than half of the students in my class are having difficulty solving two-step problems with multiplication. What ideas are there for supporting these students?"

10. **Reflect and make a SMART (specific, measurable, attainable, relevant, and timely) goal.**

    *Specific:* detailed description of what, where, when, how often, and with whom

    *Measurable:* what you will see, hear, and feel when you reach the goal

    *Attainable:* your confidence level that you can achieve the goal

    *Relevant:* the objective and purpose of the goal

    *Timely:* deadlines that are flexible and realistic (Conzemius and Morganti-Fisher 2012)

    Allow at least two minutes at the end of the collaboration time to reflect on the session. How did we learn together? Would we change anything for next time? What is our take-away? What will we do now? Make a quick SMART goal, which sounds like: I will do (what) (where) (how many times) and (by when). For example: I will use "groupable," not pregrouped, place-value models with all students during my next lesson on place value at least once by our next meeting.

# Helpful Resources for Teachers

*About Teaching Mathematics: A K–8 Resource* by Marilyn Burns (2015)

This resource provides teachers information organized into four parts: (1) Starting Points (issues to address when thinking about teaching mathematics), (2) Problem-Solving Investigations (lessons, games, and investigations that assist teachers in planning lessons for problem solving), (3) Teaching Arithmetic (ideas for understanding how students learn operations, with accompanying assessments), and (4) Questions Teachers Ask (author responses to pedagogical questions from teachers, including authentic problems of practice).

*Elementary and Middle School Mathematics: Teaching Developmentally* by John A. DeWalle, Karen S. Karp, and Jennifer M. Bay-Williams (2014)

This resource assists teachers in developing a conceptual understanding of the mathematics they will teach and the most effective methods of teaching Pre-K through eighth-grade math topics. The text uses the Common Core State Standards and the National Council for Teachers of Mathematics (NCTM) *Principles to Actions*, as well as current research, with suggestions for how to teach in a problem-based, developmentally appropriate manner that supports the learning needs of all students.

*INFORMative Assessment: Formative Assessment Practices to Improve Mathematics Achievement, Grades K–6* by Jean M. Joyner and Mari Muri (2011)

This resource describes formative assessment as an ongoing process, not a one-time event, to identify what students know and don't know. The resource includes a collection of strategies that engage teachers and students collaboratively to support students' mathematics learning. Teachers can use this resource to identify practices that elicit student thinking, and to discuss ways for teachers to implement the strategies in a manner that supports students' growth and improvement.

"Illustrative Mathematics" (www.illustrativemathematics.org)

This website provides instructional and assessment tasks that exemplify students understanding of the Common Core State Standards, lesson plans, and other resources for teachers. Resources are arranged under the Standards for Mathematical Content and for Mathematical Practices, and are organized by grade level. Use the site to identify exemplar tasks that assess student mastery of standards.

# Quick Reference Questions for Principals

In this section, we present questions we hear typically from principals as they work to lead schools that strive for continual improvement in mathematics learning. In the pages that follow, we examine how the five collaboration structures—the Strategic Planning Session, the Mathematics Content Learning Team, the Shared Classroom Experience, the Mathematics Vertical Learning Team, and the Ten-Minute Meeting—can be called on to help schools address a variety of challenges effectively.

## Overview

> Videos can be streamed by registering this product at mathsolutions.com/myvideos. See page xxiii for instructions.

## Tools You Can Use

> Tools You Can Use appear at the end of this section and are also available online at mathsolutions.com/ givemefivereproducibles.

# Give Me Five!

▶ Video Clip C.1

To view this video clip, scan the QR code or access via mathsolutions.com/ GMFC1

## From the Administrator's Perspective

*You've got to move slow to move fast. Sometimes, myself included, I'm wanting to move much quicker than we are able to move because you're talking about a whole system moving. And you can't do it by yourself. It has to take every part of that system moving to move everybody forward.*

—Evan Smith, deputy superintendent

As you watch this clip, consider the following questions:

- In what ways can you relate to what this deputy superintendent is feeling, thinking, or saying?
- What questions might you have as an administrator?

## Question 1    How can student scores improve on state assessments?

One principal shared this concern: "Students haven't shown the kind of gains we hoped. Everyone is working so hard, and we've put a lot of money, time, and resources into improving student achievement, but our data don't show gains. Why are our student scores on state assessments so low, and how can they get better?"

When we hear concerns about test scores, especially when schools have invested significantly in resources, we always look to the professional learning that is in place around mathematics. Our experience, as well as the research (Jensen et al. 2016, Johnson et al. 2013, Gallimore et al. 2009, Hill et al. 2005), has demonstrated that schools with high student scores on state assessments consistently over time enact the following practices:

- Have a shared vision, goals, and commitments for student achievement
- Ensure curriculum, instruction, and assessment are aligned across classrooms and grade levels
- Share a bank of formative assessment tools and strategies, including those involving students
- Use multiple sources of data to assess students regularly and consistently
- Collaborate to create lessons designed to advance student mastery of standards
- Provide time and structures for ongoing professional learning

- Allow for celebrations of progress, intervention, and adjustment
- Offer opportunities for teachers to analyze data collaboratively, then learn what to do differently to advance student learning

If this concern resonates with you, we recommend using the five structures listed here to establish an environment that fosters the practices listed, leading to increased student achievement and, consequently, improved test scores.

## Strategic Planning Sessions (see Chapter 1)

*How this structure helps address the question:*

- Allows the principal, math coach, and math teachers to create a shared vision for math achievement and to set common goals
- Creates an Action Plan to make the vision a reality
- Provides the opportunity to assess progress regularly and make adjustments to the Action Plan
- Creates a message of alignment between what is written (standards/curriculum), what is taught (instruction), and what is learned (assessment)

## Mathematics Content Learning Team (see Chapter 2)

*How this structure helps address the question:*

- Provides a forum for teachers to develop their math knowledge in a supportive atmosphere
- Supports collaboration and sharing of materials as well as assessment and instructional strategies
- Allows teachers to analyze student work products, determining needs and proposing solutions

## Shared Classroom Experience (see Chapter 3)

*How this structure helps address the question:*

- Allows teachers to put theory into practice, presenting lessons and evaluating student performance with peer and/or coach support
- Enables participants—which can include teachers, coaches, and/or the principal—to see how the school's vision is being implemented in the classroom

## Mathematics Vertical Learning Team (see Chapter 4)

*How this structure helps address the question:*

- Enables teachers to view progression of math skills embedded in the standards, so they can see how their objectives fit in with what students have already learned and what they are expected to learn in the future
- Helps schools identify gaps in instruction that can cause poor performance on assessments
- Supports effective lesson design and the use of common assessments
- Promotes collaboration across grade levels, which can support differentiation
- Allows for the introduction of research-based strategies to prevent conceptual gaps

**Question 2** | **What can I do to ensure all teachers teach** ......................................................
**in order to influence student learning?**

Consider this principal's concern: "I want all students in our school to have a good learning experience, which means having a good teacher. A good teacher makes all the difference in student performance, behavior, motivation, and attitude. We have some teachers that are ineffective year after year, and that must change. What can I do to ensure all teachers teach so students learn math and enjoy their learning?"

If this principal's concerns resonate with you, commit to a process of continual improvement through professional learning and growth by establishing the collaboration structures listed here.

**Strategic Planning Sessions** (see Chapter 1)

*How this structure helps address the question:*

- Allows the principal, math coach, and math teachers to create a shared vision for math achievement

- Sets goals for growth in student achievement, and creates an Action Plan for making those goals a reality

- Establishes high expectations for teacher participation in professional learning designed to improve student performance

- Clarifies everyone's roles and responsibilities

**Mathematics Content Learning Team** (see Chapter 2)

*How this structure helps address the question:*

- Conveys the expectation that all teachers are striving to improve knowledge to support student learning more effectively

- Provides a forum for teachers to develop their math knowledge in a supportive atmosphere

- Supports collaboration and sharing of materials as well as assessment and instructional strategies

- Allows teachers to analyze student work products, determining needs and proposing solutions

**Shared Classroom Experience** (see Chapter 3)

*How this structure helps address the question:*

- Provides coaches, teachers, and principals an effective way to collaborate and develop a shared mindset for teaching and student learning

- Builds shared understanding and language of effective instructional practices

- Creates a support system for teachers' changing practices

- Creates an opportunity for principals to make the message explicit: We teach so students learn. If students are not growing in their mathematics learning, we must change the way we teach math.

**Mathematics Vertical Learning Team** (see Chapter 4)

*How this structure helps address the question:*

- Provides a safe place for teachers to learn the progression of mathematical concepts

- Supports effective lesson design and use of common assessments

- Allows for the introduction of research-based strategies to prevent conceptual gaps

**Ten-Minute Meeting** (see Chapter 5)

*How this structure helps address the question:*

- Allows the principal and math coach to maintain regular communication with teachers focused on student learning

- Demonstrates that the principal values teachers' ideas and insights

- Provides time for the principal and teachers to build relationships

## Question 3    What do I do about teachers who are resistant to change?

Consider the issues challenging this principal: "This is my second year at a turnaround school. There are about three teachers who are resistant to changing their math classroom learning environment and instructional strategies. The data show it, too. Each teacher's end-of-year assessment and benchmark assessments show a decline. I'm struggling to find district support and am getting pushback from the union."

If this principal's concerns resonate with you, begin with a Ten-Minute Meeting to address three carefully crafted questions that allow you to hear teachers' point of view, address their areas of concern, and ask what support they need to improve student achievement. Arrange the schedule so all resistant teachers can be in a high-functioning professional learning structure with educators who advance thinking and learning, such as a Mathematics Content Learning Team or a Mathematics Vertical Learning Team. Meet with the coach to design a plan of support for each teacher that includes change and growth with substantive and clear documentation. Arrange for teachers to participate in a minimum of two cycles of the Shared Classroom Experience.

**Strategic Planning Sessions** (see Chapter 1)

*How this structure helps address the question:*

- Allows the principal, math coach, and teachers to create a shared vision for expectations of an effective math classroom

- Sets goals for growth in student achievement so expectations are clear to everyone

- Establishes high expectations for teacher participation in professional learning designed to improve student performance

**Mathematics Content Learning Team** (see Chapter 2)

*How this structure helps address the question:*

- Provides a forum for teachers to develop their math knowledge in a supportive atmosphere

- Supports collaboration and sharing of materials as well as assessment and instructional strategies

- Fosters shared responsibility for student learning

*(continued)*

## Give Me Five!

**Shared Classroom Experience** (see Chapter 3)

*How this structure helps address the question:*

- Builds relationships among teachers, principals, and coaches
- Allows teachers, principals, and coaches to work together to develop expertise in teaching for learning
- Supports a system for changing classroom practices that includes shared responsibility, collaboration, and sharing of materials and instructional strategies

**Mathematics Vertical Learning Team** (see Chapter 4)

*How this structure helps address the question:*

- Supports effective lesson design and use of common assessments
- Builds relationships among teachers at different grade levels
- Offers teachers a view of what will be expected of their students in the future

**Ten-Minute Meeting** (see Chapter 5)

*How this structure helps address the question:*

- Builds relational capacity
- Allows all teachers and the principal to express their vision for mathematics teaching and learning
- Elicits thinking and reasoning of teachers with regard to why scores aren't improving
- Initiates the process of providing clear expectations for growth and change
- Gives teachers a voice in shaping their own growth, and communicates the expectation of participation in a support system for change

*"What the principal deems important, the teachers deem important."*

—Courtney Blackmon, math coach

## Question 4    How can teachers across grade levels get connected? .................................

In the words of one principal: "K through two teachers don't see their role in supporting students who take state assessments in third grade. When I do classroom walks, math instruction looks different in each class, teachers use their own assessments, and our school benchmark assessments show inconsistencies. On the state assessment, third-grade scores are twenty percentage points lower than either fourth or fifth grades. I really want all K through two teachers to get on the same page with assessments and instruction so our third-grade students are well prepared to be successful on their state assessment."

If this principal's concern resonates with you, we recommend fostering professional learning and communication between grade levels by implementing the collaboration structures listed here. We also encourage you to read the message "Seek First to Understand" in *Faster Isn't Smarter* by Cathy Seeley (2015), which emphasizes: "In school settings, understanding, communicating, and working together across communities can help us generate better ways of providing every student with the highest-quality mathematics education possible" (86).

### Shared Classroom Experience (see Chapter 3)

*How this structure helps address the question:*

- Provides the opportunity for teachers to experience firsthand what their students are expected to do in future years

- Provides the opportunity for teachers to observe future students and understand how concepts are presented in previous grades

- Builds relationships among teachers at different grade levels

- Creates a shared mindset and language among teachers, coaches, and principals about math content across the grades, and about instruction that sparks student thinking and deepens understanding in all mathematics classrooms

### Mathematics Vertical Learning Team (see Chapter 4)

*How this structure helps address the question:*

- Enables teachers to view progressions of math skills embedded in the standards so they have a clear picture of where their students have come from and where they are going

- Allows teachers to determine the vocabulary they will use for math concepts so they can be consistent across the grades

- Supports effective lesson design and the use of common assessments

- Promotes collaboration across grade levels, which can support differentiation

| Question 5 | **How can teachers collaborate effectively** |
| --- | --- |
| | **so our school culture is less toxic?** |

Consider the situation faced by this principal: "Our school culture is toxic. What I mean by this is teachers spend a lot of time blaming students and parents for school performance, and it feels fragmented and unproductive. It feels like we are here for the adults and not the students. This is my second year as a principal. During my first year, I didn't want to rock the boat. I treated teachers as professionals and honored their decisions about topics for collaboration time. But, little is changing in the way teachers talk with each other. Talk is not about students, or teaching and learning; it's about why students aren't performing. This must change. How can the teachers at our school collaborate more effectively to create a positive school culture for learning?"

If this principal's concerns resonate with you, consider the following strategies used by principals that have been effective in shifting school cultures from toxic to positive (Pearson and Deal 1998):

- Building trust and professional relationships through conversations
- Communicating the school's vision, mission, and values
- Modeling how to talk together
- Focusing talk on students
- Using talk to question and explore a situation rather than just to explain the current state of things. For example, one teacher explains, "Our students aren't motivated." The principal asks, "How can they get motivated? What strategies are used by teachers to motivate students?"
- Using multiple sources of data to focus talk on students
- Creating a shared vision, goals, commitments, and mindsets for student achievement
- Identifying multiple ways to achieve goals
- Providing time and structures for ongoing professional learning in a safe environment— one where teachers are not allowed to sabotage new ideas
- Allowing for recognition through exemplars of practice

  As principal, your role is to fulfill three tasks of leadership (Wallace Foundation 2013):

- Shape a vision of academic success for all students
- Initiate and convene conversations that shift people's experiences toward improving instruction
- Cultivate leadership in others

The five collaboration structures listed here can be used throughout the school year to implement these strategies and help you fulfill your leadership tasks.

### Strategic Planning Sessions (see Chapter 1)

*How this structure helps address the question:*

- Allows faculty to develop norms for collaboration so the principal, math coach, and teachers can work productively together
- Gives everyone a voice in the school's direction
- Provides an opportunity for the principal, math coach, and teachers to create a shared vision for math achievement and to set common goals
- Creates an Action Plan to make the vision a reality
- Keeps the focus on student learning

### Mathematics Content Learning Team (see Chapter 2)

*How this structure helps address the question:*

- Provides a forum for teachers to develop their math knowledge in a supportive atmosphere
- Supports collaboration and sharing of materials as well as assessment and instructional strategies
- Develops a strong, student-focused culture

### Shared Classroom Experience (see Chapter 3)

*How this structure helps address the question:*

- Builds relationships among teachers, coach, and principal
- Strengthens teachers' relationships with students in other classes; reconnects them with former students and/or introduces them to potential students

- Allows teachers to develop their knowledge and skills collaboratively for teaching math, resulting in increased student engagement
- Creates shared language and mindsets for effective instruction, along with an opportunity to generate solutions among teachers, coach, and principal

### Mathematics Vertical Learning Team (see Chapter 4)

*How this structure helps address the question:*

- Builds relationships and promotes collaboration among teachers at different grade levels
- Supports effective lesson design and use of common assessments
- Develops a strong, student-focused culture

### Ten-Minute Meeting (see Chapter 5)

*How this structure helps address the question:*

- Serves as a quick, doable touchpoint—a point of contact between two people that facilitates communication
- Promotes autonomy; anyone can initiate a Ten-Minute Meeting to clarify a task and/or voice a concern
- Serves as a proactive move to diffuse confusion, doubt, fear, and anger; the Ten-Minute Meeting "Three Questions" (Reproducible 27) are a safe way to clear up misunderstandings and assumptions, and can keep communication lines open

**How do I ensure math achievement is not compromised** .......................... **when budgets have been cut drastically?**

One principal wrestled with these circumstances: "Our budgets are cut. I'm losing the assistant principal, four teachers, and three teaching assistants. Class sizes will increase. After-school tutorials have been eliminated. We don't have money to purchase new technology or math resources for teachers and students. It seems impossible to maintain our increases in students' math achievement with such a reduction in resources."

If this concern resonates with you, be assured that students' math achievement can continue to grow if collaboration structures are in place to support teachers. Research tells us that when teachers work in teams to identify common student needs, design lessons with an instructional focus, teach the lesson in the classroom, analyze student work, then revise and redesign the lesson—all with the principal's support—student achievement increases (Saunders et al. 2009). The four structures listed here provide the support teachers need to continue improving math achievement.

**Strategic Planning Sessions** (see Chapter 1)

*How this structure helps address the question:*

- Empowers teachers by giving them a voice in how to improve students' math achievement

- Allows the principal, math coach, and math teachers to create a shared vision for math achievement and to set common goals

- Creates an Action Plan to make the vision a reality, so everybody understands what they need to do to effect continued growth in mathematics achievement

**Mathematics Content Learning Team** (see Chapter 2)

*How this structure helps address the question:*

- Provides a forum for teachers to develop their math knowledge in a supportive atmosphere

- Supports collaboration and sharing of materials as well as assessment and instructional strategies, which is particularly helpful when budgets prevent attending conferences or other professional development activities

**Shared Classroom Experience** (see Chapter 3)

*How this structure helps address the question:*

- Builds relationships among teachers, principals, and coaches

- Creates a support system for teachers in the process of changing instructional practices

- Gives teachers an extra set of eyes in the classroom to help diagnose student learning needs and problem areas

- Supports collaboration and sharing of materials as well as assessment and instructional strategies

**Mathematics Vertical Learning Team** (see Chapter 4)

*How this structure helps address the question:*

- Helps schools identify gaps in instruction that can cause poor performance on assessments

- Supports effective lesson design and use of common assessments

- Builds relationships and promotes collaboration among teachers at different grade levels

---

**Question 7** — **What can I do to support new math coaches so they are effective in bolstering student and teacher learning?**

One principal expressed this concern: "Our math coach retired. What a loss! She had good rapport with the teachers. Student achievement improved during the past two years. Now, a first-year coach who's been teaching middle school has been assigned to our school to replace her. With no money for the coach's professional development or time to 'catch up,' what can I do to support the new math coach so she is effective in supporting student and teacher learning?"

If this principal's concern resonates with you, use the two collaboration structures listed here to clarify the coach's role, to communicate your expectations, and to establish and maintain regular communication throughout the year. Encourage the coach to spend the first month building rapport with teachers by listening to them and asking questions about practices that work to support students. We also recommend you share this resource with the coach, particularly Chapter 2.

**Strategic Planning Sessions** (see Chapter 1)

*How this structure helps address the question:*

- Allows the principal, math coach, and teachers to create a shared vision for math achievement and to set common goals

- Offers the opportunity to address the questions and concerns teachers and the coach have about working together, such as
  —What does the math coach do here at our school?
  —Why do we have a math coach?
  —How does the math coach work collaboratively with everyone?
  — How do we ensure the coach is seen as part of the team and not separate with a higher status?
  —Who works with the math coach? When?
  —How do we all learn together as partners in supporting student achievement?

- Provides a focus and direction for the coach

- Builds a support system for the coach

**Ten-Minute Meeting** (see Chapter 5)

*How this structure helps address the question:*

- Creates a regular touchpoint of contact between the principal and coach

- Allows the coach to clarify his or her role

- Provides time to discuss issues regularly, before they become problems

## Question 8    What happens when the math coach position is eliminated?

One principal shared this situation: "Our school lost the math coach. State funding was reduced and all math coaching positions were eliminated. Who will support the teachers to ensure student achievement? What will we do without a math coach?"

If this principal's concern resonates with you, focus on developing collaboration and teacher leadership among your teachers using the structures listed here. Improved student learning occurs as a result of daily collaboration between and among teachers (Ronfeldt et al. 2015). Strong teacher leadership can propel teacher collaboration and learning, which in turn impacts student growth. Teacher leadership involves teachers leading beyond the classroom, identifying with and contributing to a community of teacher learners, and influencing others toward improved educational practice (Katzenmeyer and Moller 2009).

### Strategic Planning Sessions (see Chapter 1)

*How this structure helps address the question:*

- Allows the principal, teacher leaders, and teachers time to regroup and reorganize when a key position is eliminated

- Enables educators to envision how professional learning will continue without the role of the coach

- Creates an Action Plan to make that vision a reality

### Mathematics Content Learning Team (see Chapter 2)

*How this structure helps address the question:*

- Provides a forum for teachers to develop their math knowledge in a supportive atmosphere

- Supports collaboration and sharing of materials as well as assessment and instructional strategies

### Shared Classroom Experience (see Chapter 3)

*How this structure helps address the question:*

- Builds relationships among teachers

- Allows teachers and principals to work together to develop expertise in teaching for learning

- Provides a system to support changing classroom practices that includes collaboration and sharing of materials and instructional strategies

### Mathematics Vertical Learning Team (see Chapter 4)

*How this structure helps address the question:*

- Helps schools identify gaps in instruction that can cause poor performance on assessments

- Supports effective lesson design and use of common assessments

- Builds relationships and promotes collaboration among teachers at different grade levels

| Question 9 | What happens when a new key leader introduces ............................ a new and different agenda for math teaching? |
| --- | --- |

One principal shared this dilemma: "We have a new curriculum director who wants to make changes in the curriculum and bring in a program unfamiliar to our teachers. It worked in her district, and now she wants to bring it here. Our former director was most helpful in getting teachers onboard with the curriculum scope and sequence, and providing professional development for all teachers using the same resources and common assessments. Our test scores show it; they have been improving steadily. I don't want to ask teachers to make any major changes in the math program. I'd like them to stay the course and maintain momentum. How can the momentum continue without major changes?"

If this principal's concerns resonate with you, be proactive. Introduce yourself and your leadership team as soon as possible, and share your vision for your school and your current path for achieving that vision. We recommend conducting a Ten-Minute Meeting for this initial discussion, then follow up with a Strategic Planning Session, and continue Ten-Minute Meetings throughout the year to maintain communication.

**Strategic Planning Sessions** (see Chapter 1)

*How this structure helps address the question:*

- Allows the new leader, principal, and leadership team time to create a shared vision for the district and/or school's mathematics program
- Enables educators to clarify expectations for the curriculum—standards, resources, textbook, and the type of instruction and assessment that teachers should use
- Creates an Action Plan to make that vision a reality

**Ten-Minute Meeting** (see Chapter 5)

*How this structure helps address the question:*

- Provides a manageable block of time for focused discussion that is easy to fit into the busiest of schedules
- Allows leadership teams to express their vision and path accompanied by data that show evidence of results and growth for the past few years
- Elicits thinking and reasoning of the new leader
- Initiates the process of getting on the same page and creating shared agreements
- Builds rapport

**Question 10** **What kind of feedback can I give teachers that is meaningful** ..................... **and useful, and creates changes to their math instruction?**

A principal who recently received results from a teacher survey said, "Our recent midyear survey data indicate teachers want feedback that will help them create changes in their math instruction. I haven't been able to get into classrooms as much I would like, and I'm not sure what type of feedback they are asking for."

If this principal's concern resonates with you, start by attending Mathematics Vertical and Content Learning Team meetings. Listen to the teachers' conversations to understand more completely the knowledge and skills teachers are developing. The content you hear will help you know how to align your feedback to advance what teachers are learning during the team meetings. A Ten-Minute Meeting and Shared Classroom Experience also serve to help you and the teachers get on the same page with feedback, and offer opportunities to practice feedback skills.

### Mathematics Content
### Learning Team (see Chapter 2)

*How this structure helps address the question:*

- Provides a forum for the principal to share feedback "themes" that need to be addressed across the grade level, such as asking effective questions to elicit student thinking

- Supports collaboration, solution finding, and sharing responsibility for addressing feedback "themes"

- Allows the principal to ask teachers which types of feedback would be most useful to advance their learning and changing practices in the classroom

### Shared Classroom Experience (see Chapter 3)

*How this structure helps address the question:*

- Allows teachers and principals to work together to develop expertise in teaching for learning

- Offers an opportunity to reflect together on the lesson and discuss areas related to the feedback "themes"

### Mathematics Vertical
### Learning Team (see Chapter 4)

*How this structure helps address the question:*

- Allows a structure and time for the principal to share feedback "themes" noticed across all grade levels, such as posing depth of knowledge questions that increase rigor in student thinking

- Supports shared responsibility and ownership for addressing solutions to the feedback

- Promotes increased communication across grade levels

- Allows the principal to ask teachers which types of feedback would be most useful to advance their learning and changing practices in the classroom

**Ten-Minute Meeting** (see Chapter 5)

*How this structure helps address the question:*

- Provides a manageable block of time for focused feedback that is easy to fit into the busiest of schedules

- Allows the teacher and principal time to engage in a reciprocal exchange of feedback, where the principal initiates three questions to provide feedback, then both teacher and principal engage in conversation about the feedback

- Elicits thinking and reasoning of both principal and teachers to find effective solutions that address feedback for change and improvements

- Assists the principal in understanding teachers' needs, and helps teachers understand the principal's intention and purpose for the feedback

- Builds shared understanding of instructional goals

### Ten Tips for Leading within a Culture of Professional Growth and Collaboration

As you work to establish or maintain a collaborative school culture dedicated to professional learning and student growth, keep in mind the following tips.

1. **Communicate your purpose, expectations, and overall vision clearly.** Teachers want what's best for their students and are generally happy to learn new ways to improve their practice. However, they do not like being given directives without reasons and without the opportunity to provide input. As you address difficult issues and communicate about new professional learning structures and programs, be sure to tie the discussion to everyone's common goal: improving student achievement in mathematics.

2. **Foster collaborative communication by adopting norms.** As teachers—or any group of adults—strive to work together, having a set of guidelines for how to interact productively can make discussing even the most difficult issues manageable. See the discussion on page 58 in Part II, Chapter 1 for one way to establish norms during professional meetings.

3. **Deepen people's communication skills.** Talk is powerful. It can guide people toward change, or it can simply maintain the status quo. Some verbal behaviors lead to the generation of new ideas and solutions to problems of practice; others serve just to keep things the same. Increase awareness of the paths of talk and listen for statements that cause the situation to remain the same (*My students don't know their basic facts.*) and statements that generate solutions (*What strategies can be used so students learn their basic facts with understanding, and retain their basic facts year after year?*). Encourage teachers and coaches to reframe status quo statements with those that spur problem solving and goal setting.

4. **Nurture distributed leadership.** If leadership is, fundamentally, about influencing change, then this influence is not confined to positions of authority. Encourage and stimulate the leadership capability and strengths of all educators to realize desired outcomes and results. Mobilizing leadership expertise at all levels of the system—coaches, teacher leaders, and teachers—builds capacity for change and improvement.

5. **Provide time; create schedules.** For teachers to work together productively, they need time set aside exclusively for that purpose. Time is a precious commodity during the school day, but as a principal, you have power over the schedule; you can schedule time for regular professional learning meetings, such as Mathematics Content Learning Teams and Mathematics Vertical Learning Teams, and make arrangements, such as using paraprofessionals or substitutes, so that teachers can have a common planning time to plan for Shared Classroom Experience.

6. **Address people's concerns.** As teachers participate in the various learning structures, listen closely to their concerns about participating in the structure. Whatever the concern, find a way to listen without judgment, and provide suggestions for successful participation. For example, if teachers are concerned about having other educators in their classroom for a Shared Classroom Experience, assure them that student learning is the focus of all conversations and that individual teachers will not be critiqued under any circumstances.

7. **Protect meeting agendas.** Competing priorities often make it tempting to refocus a meeting. Resist. Professional learning meetings are essential for building teacher expertise and improving student achievement. In the long term, nothing is more important than those goals. It's important for teachers to know their learning will not be interrupted with other issues, such as sharing test data or highlighting management concerns.

8. **Attend three to four meetings per year.** As principal, you have many obligations that make it impossible to attend every professional learning meeting in your school. Yet, demonstrating your commitment to teachers and their learning is key to any school improvement plan. Make it a priority to attend three or four of each type of meeting per year, staying at least ten minutes each time. This action shows you value teachers' learning and appreciate their commitment and hard work. Just "showing up," listening attentively, and asking a question of interest sends a valuable message: *This is important. You are valued.*

9. **Monitor and reflect on implementation.** It's important to keep apprised of the learning going on during the school year. We recommend requiring each team to keep a record of their learning and to send it to you via email after each meeting. Alternatively, teams can keep a hard copy in a notebook that you review periodically. At faculty meetings, take a few minutes to ask each team to share how the meetings are going, considering the questions: *What's working? What's not? What do we keep doing? What do we stop doing?*

10. **Acknowledge hard work and effort toward professional learning.** Acknowledge— verbally, via an email, or in a short handwritten note—your appreciation of everyone's efforts. Teaching is a challenging and often thankless job, so showing your support and approval of teachers' efforts goes a long way toward boosting morale and keeping motivation high.

# Helpful Resources for Principals

*Leading the Way: Principals and Superintendents Look at Math Instruction* by Marilyn Burns (1998)

This collection of essays provides a look at the challenges administrators face and the actions they've taken to promote effective mathematics education for all students. Superintendents, principals, math coordinators, teacher leaders, math coaches, and other administrators who are supporting high-quality, standards-based mathematics instruction in their schools and districts will find the contents and practical strategies useful for promoting quality mathematics teaching and learning.

*Faster Isn't Smarter: Messages About Math Teaching and Learning in the 21st Century*, Second Edition by Cathy Seeley (2015)

This resource features clear messages about some of today's most important, essential issues in mathematics education. The themes range from equity, intelligence, and the potential of all students, to challenging students to think with a problem-centered approach, which is focused on engaging students through classroom discourse. The resource provides a base for thoughtful discussion among elementary, middle, and high school teachers, leaders, policymakers, and families.

*The School Principal as Leader: Guiding Schools to Better Teaching and Learning* by the Wallace Foundation (2013)

This Wallace *Perspective* summarizes ten years of foundation research and work in school leadership to identify what effective school principals do. It concludes that they carry out five key actions particularly well, including shaping a vision of academic success for all students and cultivating leadership in others. The resource is an expanded edition of a report published originally in 2012.

*Elementary and Middle School Mathematics: Teaching Developmentally* by John A. Van DeWalle, Karen S. Karp, and Jennifer M. Bay-Williams (2014)

This best-selling book guides teachers in supporting all Pre-K–8 learners in making sense of math by supporting their own mathematical understanding and effective planning and instruction. Every teacher needs access to this book when planning instruction. If it is not possible financially for every teacher to have a copy, then ensure every grade level has access to this resource during collaborative planning time.

# Part II

# The Five Collaboration Structures

In this part, we detail how to implement each collaboration structure so you get what you need up and running in your school or district. We share video clips of the structures in action, provide step-by-step guidelines for implementation, and offer tools and templates to support your work. You'll also find stories from real teachers and administrators who have used the structures effectively and have seen professional learning and math achievement soar. We encourage you to take time to reflect on the "Your Turn" questions and prompts, and use them to spur action in your school. Together, you and your colleagues have the power to effect real change—and make a real difference in students' mathematics success.

## Overview

# Chapter 1

# Strategic Planning Sessions

Implementing change begins with a vision. For mathematics instruction and achievement to improve, teachers and administrators must create a shared vision, developing similar mindsets and committing to actions and behaviors that can lead to mathematics success. The foundation of this process is the Strategic Planning Session.

In this chapter, we outline how to plan and implement successful Strategic Planning Sessions. We

- Offer a video clip of an actual session in practice

- Provide step-by-step guidelines for running the sessions

- Share tools, agendas, and templates for enacting sessions throughout the school year

- Suggest strategies for ensuring a successful session

- Describe variations at both the school and district levels

We end the chapter with a "Your Turn" that gives you an opportunity to start designing your own Strategic Planning Sessions.

## Overview

## Tools You Can Use

Videos can be streamed by registering this product at mathsolutions.com/myvideos. See page xxiii for instructions.

Tools You Can Use (Reproducibles) appear at the end of the chapter and are also available online at mathsolutions.com/ givemefivereproducibles.com.

# How It Looks in Practice

Pampa Independent School District holds their district-level Strategic Planning Session 3 at the end of the school year in May. Fifteen professionals from four elementary schools and the administration participate in the three-hour session, including teachers, math coaches, teacher leaders, and principals. The session is led by Janice Bradley, a professional learning consultant who has been facilitating change in the district and who is a coauthor of this book.

**▶ Video Clip 1.1**

To view this video clip, scan the QR code or access via mathsolutions.com/GMF11

## A Strategic Planning Session in Action

As you watch this clip featuring excerpts from Pampa Independent School District's Strategic Planning Session 3, consider the following questions:

- What elements of the session strike you as important or beneficial? Why?
- What do you notice about how participants work together?
- How does the session compare with meetings in which you have participated, either at the school level or the district level?
- What happened during the session that you would like to see happen in your district or school? Why?

See the authors' reflections on these questions in the Appendix.

**Your Turn** | Defining a Strategic Planning Session

Think about words that come to mind when you hear the term *strategic planning session*. If you haven't attended such a meeting, you might wonder what it is and why you should participate. Consider what would be the ideal of such a meeting. What words come to mind? List some of the words that come to mind here:

_____

_____

_____

Based on ideas gleaned from the video clip, write a definition in your own words of a Strategic Planning Session.

_____

_____

_____

_____

_____

# What Is a Strategic Planning Session?

## The Equation

Strategic—designed carefully to serve a particular purpose

$+$

Planning—make preparations for specific actions to occur in the future

$+$

Session—meet to promote shared visions, goals, and commitments

$=$

Mathematical Success

## The Definition

A Strategic Planning Session is a meeting during which district leaders/administrators, principals, teachers, math coaches, teacher leaders, and teachers plan for systemic change in math instruction. They share a Vision Statement, envisioning mathematics classrooms designed to support student learning. They also share an Action Plan to achieve that vision. The Action Plan is implemented through the collaboration structures detailed in this resource: the Mathematics Content Learning Team (Chapter 2), the Shared Classroom Experience (Chapter 3), and the Mathematics Vertical Learning Team (Chapter 4). The outcome for each Strategic Planning Session is to transform imagined changes into real changes.

❝The outcome of each Strategic Planning Session is to transform imagined changes into real changes.❞

. . . . . . . . . . . . . . . . . . . . . . . . . . . . . . . . . . . . . . . . . . . . . . . . . . . . . . . . . . . . . . . . .

## Research Says . . .

There is compelling evidence from a core set of practices leaders call on to improve student learning. One practice—the Strategic Planning Session—is used in organizations from business to government to education to create change and improvements. In government, a Strategic Planning Meeting refers to the current state of collective thinking about what the future might be like (Gordon 2013).

Strategic Planning Meetings are also used extensively in public and nonprofit organizations to imagine changes, to clarify the vision and goals for change, use data to identify the current state and root causes of problems, to formulate a strategy for change, and to design a plan to implement and monitor the change (Bryson 2011).

The purpose of each meeting is to look at the future in a coherent, systemic way. There is broad agreement among leaders and experts in education that planning is an essential component for managing and realizing effective change. A Strategic Planning Session is an organization's process of defining a plan of action to reach a goal. Think of this session as a tool for organizing the present based on projections of the desired future. It is a road map for where a school wants to be one, three, or five years from now. Strategic Planning Sessions are doable, manageable, and easy to implement, with substantial payoffs for a minimal time investment.

In addition, Strategic Planning Sessions support professional learning, which in turn impacts student achievement. Intentional and purposefully designed learning for adults produces better outcomes for students (Hord and Hirsch 2008). Strategic Planning Sessions provide an opportunity for actions toward outcomes to be intentional, and for learning to occur more deeply and richly through interactions and conversations that allow staff members to pursue intentional learning, share new knowledge, test ideas, ask questions, gain clarification, debate conclusions, and seek consensus on how to transfer new learning to practice.

. . . . . . . . . . . . . . . . . . . . . . . . . . . . . . . . . . . . . . . . . . . . . . . . . . . . . . . . . . . . . . . . .

# Scheduling Strategic Planning Sessions

We recommend that Strategic Planning Sessions occur annually, three times at the district level and, for each school involved, three times at the school level. This will ensure a systemic, ongoing process of continuous improvement. Each of the three district-level sessions should include district leaders, principals, and a key math coach and teacher from each elementary campus. Each of the three school-level sessions (per school) should include the key math coach and teacher who attended the district-level session, the school's principal, and at minimum a teacher from every grade level. These school-level teams might also be referred to as Math Leadership Teams. The meetings transpire as follows:

### Session 1:  Creating a Shared Vision and Making an Action Plan

This session happens at the beginning of the school year, typically in August. First, professionals meet for two to three hours at a district level to create a District Vision Statement and Action Plan, then campus representatives (the key math coach and teacher who attended the district-level session) facilitate a one-hour session at the school level (with the school's Math Leadership Team) to ensure the campus' vision and actions for improvement of mathematics teaching and learning are aligned with the District Vision Statement.

### Session 2:  Assessing Impact and Addressing Challenges

This session happens midway through the school year, typically in December or January. First, campus representatives (the key math coach and teacher) facilitate a one-hour session at the school level (with the school's Math Leadership Team) to review data and results of actions. Then they share this information in a two- to three-hour district-level session.

### Session 3:  Acknowledging Progress and Planning for Continuous Improvement

This session happens at the end of the school year, typically in May or early June. First, campus representatives (the key math coach and teacher) facilitate a one-hour session at the school level (with the school's Math Leadership Team) to review data and results of actions. Then they share this information in a two- to three-hour district-level session.

This session cycle repeats annually as part of an ongoing, continuous improvement plan.

Before Session 1, the district math supervisor or other educator leading the initiative for math improvement schedules a half-hour meeting with key leaders (representatives of the central office, math coaches, and principals) to agree on the purposes of the Strategic Planning Sessions and calendar each one. The group should be prepared to answer these questions:

- What changes do we envision in mathematics instruction?
- What are Strategic Planning Sessions and how will they help make these changes a reality?
- Who should be present at each Strategic Planning Session?
- When can we meet?

For a tips on inviting participants, including a sample invitation, see page 81.

See Steps 1 and 2 in Reproducible 1: Ten-Step Guide to Strategic Planning Sessions (page 89).

Together, this group identifies the participants (district leaders, principals, and a key math coach and math teacher from each school) and sets the date and time for each of the three district-level Strategic Planning Sessions. The dates, times, and locations are entered on the calendar district employees use. Then the school-level sessions are calendared (three sessions for each school). For Strategic Planning Session 1, the school-level session should happen within two weeks after the district-level session. For Strategic Planning Sessions 2 and 3, the school-level sessions should happen within two weeks before the district-level sessions. The principal or key math coach from each school then sends out invitations to the teachers at their school (a minimum of one teacher per grade level). A few days before each session email reminders should also be sent.

## Your Turn

Imagine talking with an administrator, math coach/teacher leader, and teacher at your school. How would each of you respond to the following questions? Would you each have a similar response?

- Where are we going?
- What are we trying?
- How is it working?
- What needs to change?
- What needs to keep happening?

How might a Strategic Planning Session help educators at your school develop similar mindsets and goals?

# What Is the Agenda for Each Strategic Planning Session?

Each Strategic Planning Session has a different objective designed to facilitate a district's learning pathway for change using a process of continuous improvement. Learning is documented at each meeting and is used to build knowledge of content and instructional practice. The following pages provide step-by-step guidelines for implementing each of the sessions.

## Session 1 Creating a Shared Vision and Making an Action Plan

**Approximate Time**    District level: 2–3 hours; School level: 1 hour

**Scheduling**    This session occurs before the school year starts, typically in August. First, professionals meet at a district level, then campus representatives (the key math coach and teacher who attended the district-level session) facilitate a session at the school level within two weeks after the district-level sesson.

See Reproducible 1, Ten-Step Guide to Strategic Planning Sessions, on page 89.

See Reproducible 2: Strategic Planning Session 1 Agenda (Key Questions) on page 92.

### Objectives

- Establish norms for collaboration.

- Set the direction for learning by creating a shared vision— the Vision Statement.

- Create a snapshot of what is happening in math classrooms at present and identify areas to strengthen.

- Create an Action Plan for how to support professional learning connected to student learning.

- Specify who will implement the actions; include calendaring.

| Step | Documents to Create | |
|------|---------------------|---|
| | *District Level* | *School Level* |
| Step 1: Where are we going? | Vision Statement: reflects district's vision | Vision Statement: reflects school's vision and aligns with district's |
| | Current Realities Chart | Current Realities Chart |
| Step 2: How will we get there? | Action Plan: sets one to three SMART goals to move toward vision | Action Plan: provides details on how schools will meet SMART goals set in the District Action Plan |
| | Roles and Responsibilities Chart: details who is responsible for each goal on the District Action Plan | Roles and Responsibilities Chart: details who is responsible for each goal on the School Action Plan |
| Step 3: Who will do what and when, and how will we assess the impact? | Calendar: includes dates and times of three district-level sessions | Calendar: includes all professional learning activities in Action Plan |

## Step 1: Where Are We Going? (45–60 minutes)

### At the district . . .

*Objective: Establish norms for collaboration*

After brief introductions, the facilitator begins by discussing the collaborative intention of the Strategic Planning Session: to work together to find ways of improving student mathematics learning. The facilitator uses a protocol to guide the group in setting norms. The protocol has three parts:

For tips for successful facilitation, see Reproducible 7, Tips for Successful Facilitation, on page 98.

**A. Set a Productive Tone.** The facilitator begins by saying something like, "We want meetings to be efficient, relevant, and productive so we can make a real difference for the students in our classrooms. How do we behave so we make good use of our time, so that we ensure our time is used efficiently and not wasted?" Each person in the group shares behaviors that will and will not lead to productive learning conversations. The facilitator lists each person's ideas, such as using the cell phone and computer wisely, and using technology strategically for learning.

> **Key Question**
>
> • How can we work productively together?

**B. Use Norms.** Next, the facilitator asks, "How can we use norms to ensure we learn during our time together?" The facilitator offers a list of seven norms for collaboration (see the following section), providing brief descriptions to the group, and asks each person to take a moment and think about what each norm means. The facilitator might prompt, "Pick one norm that interests you. What does it mean? Will it be easy or challenging for you to use?"

For tips on how to encourage full participation, see Reproducible 8, Tips for Successful Collaboration on page 99.

**C. Reach Consensus.** The facilitator brings group members to consensus about the norms they will adopt, saying something such as, "Could we use these seven norms during our Strategic Planning Sessions? How could using the norms support our work? Is there a downside to using the norms? Can we agree to use this set of norms?" Document group norms so they can be referred to in subsequent meetings.

For suggestions on how to get a group to reach consensus, see page 84.

## Seven Norms of Collaboration

These norms were developed by educators Robert Garmston and Bruce Wellman to promote learning through collaboration. They have been used successfully in education, government, and corporate settings because they help people communicate effectively. As Garmston and Wellman (2009) state, "When the seven norms of collaborative work become an established part of a group, cohesion, energy and commitment to shared work and to the group increase dramatically" (31). For this reason, we recommend introducing and using these norms in any collaborative professional learning situation.

1. **Pausing.** Pausing is the same as wait time and it is used for the same reason in adult interactions as it is in the classroom. People need time to think after a question is asked. Pausing gives time for reflection or time to organize thoughts into a coherent and complete response. Pausing also signifies to others their ideas and comments are worth thinking about; it also encourages participation.

*(continued)*

# Give Me Five!

2. **Paraphrasing.** Paraphrasing means restating an idea using different words to clarify or confirm a speaker's meaning. For instance, "So what you are saying is that your students have trouble 'keeping track' when they are counting?"

3. **Putting Inquiry at the Center.** Asking questions opens up people's thinking and encourages a wide range of responses. So, begin with a question rather than a statement of opinion or belief, then really listen before advocating a particular idea. This approach leads to more productive discussions. For example, rather than beginning with a preferred method of instruction, ask "How can we increase students' understanding of fraction operations? What kinds of models will increase students' conceptual understanding?" to invite everyone to participate and share ideas.

4. **Probing for Specificity.** Continue asking questions to clarify something that is not fully understood or to push beyond generalizations by asking for specific details. "None of my students understood the lesson" could be followed by "Where does their problem solving break down?" Or, "Let's look as some examples of student work to see if we can identify where their thinking went off track." These probes help participants focus on the problem and work toward understanding.

5. **Placing Ideas on the Table.** Ideas that are withheld and not spoken or written do not help the group. To be an effective team, everyone should feel open and free to contribute their ideas. Ideas are also needed to be taken off the table when they are no longer relevant or when the idea has been addressed.

6. **Paying Attention to Self and Others.** This norm encourages all participants to be mindful of what they are saying, including body language. Be aware of how others are receiving your message and how you are listening or responding to others. Pay attention to different learning styles. Some people are task oriented and want to get things completed quickly, some want to see the big picture, some want to know the "why," others are concerned with the details of the situation, and still others are focused on how people feel. By knowing each person's style, each person can participate more fully—and should allow others the same courtesy.

7. **Presuming Positive Intentions.** The main purpose of the team is student learning, and all participants should assume that is everyone's goal. Encourage honest conversations so the team can be as effective as possible. Avoid inferring negative intent and always assume others' intentions are positive.

## Key Question

- What vision do we have or what changes do we want to see to improve student learning one to three years from now?

*Objective: Set the direction for learning by creating a shared vision* (Vision Statement)

When the norms have been established, the facilitator turns to the question: Where are we going? Participants should then think about what they want to see in an effective math classroom, posing questions such as

*In an effective math classroom . . .*

- How is the physical environment arranged?
- What is the teacher doing? What are the students doing?
- How will students be engaged cognitively in learning math standards?
- Are learning objectives visible and understood by students?
- What is the evidence of student learning?

This exercise can be done as a large group as a brainstorming exercise, with someone recording responses on chart paper or a digital device (if the screen can be projected). See an example of a chart on page 71. If the number of group members is more than ten, participants can work in small groups by campus, with each group making a chart and sharing it with the whole group at the end. As each group shares, other groups place a check mark by the characteristic if they also have it listed, and the facilitator creates a master list containing all agreed-to items. The end result is the initial Vision Statement. The whole group then consults their state standards to see how well the descriptors in the Vision Statement match the standards-based vision of an effective mathematics classroom, adjusting the Vision Statement as necessary. The revised chart becomes the district's Vision Statement—a document that describes the ideal mathematics learning environment the district wants to achieve. It should be posted for the whole group to see. A sample of a district vision statement might be:

### District Vision Statement

Every day, students will be engaged in rich math tasks that allow them to develop understanding of Standards' core content through mathematical practices. The teacher poses interesting and challenging questions, while the students are highly engaged in solving problems.

> For ideas on how to help participants create as vivid a vision as possible, see Reproducible 5, Developing a Vision Statement (page 95).

### Objective: Create a snapshot of what is happening in math classrooms at present and identify areas to strengthen (Current Realities Chart)

Participants then return to their campus groups and answer the same questions listed earlier based on what a typical classroom currently looks like in their school. Each group writes these characteristics on a Current Realities Chart, which serves as a snapshot of what is happening in math classrooms at this point in time. Comparing these charts with the Vision Statement will help each campus develop a plan to achieve the vision. Examples of items that participants share while putting together this chart could be:

- Students are working quietly and independently on worksheets most of the math time.
- The teacher demonstrates one way to do a problem, and students practice that method.
- Once students begin working independently, most struggle and need intervention.
- Students do very little speaking about their solutions, and have minimal interactions with other students.

- Initial instruction is ineffective in providing opportunities for students to master a concept or skill.
- Math scores show the lowest proficiency rates are about fractions and solving non-routine word problems.

## At the school . . .

Schools may choose to replicate the process used at the district-level session, or one of the campus representatives (the key math coach or teacher) who attended the district-level session can present the results of the exercise. If schools create their own Vision Statement, the facilitator should ensure it aligns with the district vision. At the end of this step, campus faculty should have the opportunity to discuss the Vision Statement and Current Realities Chart in preparation for Step 2.

## Research Says . . .

According to a review of research from the Learning from Leadership Project on how leadership influences student learning, evidence suggests that setting direction accounts for the largest proportion of leaders' impact (Louis et al. 2010).

**Key Question**

- What one to three actions need to be taken in the current semester to move us toward our vision?

## Step 2:  How Will We Get There? (30–45 minutes)

### At the district . . .

*Objective:  Create an Action Plan for how to support professional learning connected to student learning*

During this step, participants create an Action Plan that outlines steps to take to move toward the Vision Statement. At this point, it is helpful for a facilitator to present the collaborative structures schools can use to implement their Action Plans. If participants are familiar with these structures, a quick review should suffice; otherwise, the facilitator can introduce each one and describe briefly how it works:

**Collaborative Structures for Learning**

**Mathematics Content Learning Team:** Grade-level teachers meet together to focus on how students understand the math content in their grade level. They deepen their mathematics content knowledge needed for teaching, share materials and strategies, and analyze student work and behaviors to understand more completely student thinking about mathematics (see Chapter 2 for more details).

**Shared Classroom Experience:** This structure allows teachers to plan and teach a lesson together in one of their classrooms in collaboration with a math coach and/or the principal, then debrief on the process (see Chapter 3 for more details).

**Mathematics Vertical Learning Team:** Teachers from different grade levels meet to deepen their knowledge of the vertical learning progression of mathematic concepts, and share instructional strategies and assessment tools (see Chapter 4 for more details).

At the district-level session, participants may decide to set broad goals or directives for each school to address in their school-level session. For example, if test scores reveal that fractions are a weakness, a broad goal might be to strategize how to improve instruction and student learning of fractions. Alternatively, campus teams may design their own specific Action Plans to present to their corresponding schools. For instance, one campus group might plan to implement Mathematics Content Learning Teams to meet twice a month to discuss instruction of fractions, paired with Shared Classroom Experiences in which teachers plan and teach lessons for working with fractions using strategies for emergent bilingual students. In any event, the goals should be SMART: specific, measurable, attainable, relevant, and timely. These characteristics make the actions seem doable and allow for them to be evaluated easily at the next meeting. We recommend limiting the number of goals to three; this is a manageable number to which educators can commit. (See Figure 1–1 on page 64 for a sample of a District Action Plan; also see the photographed Action Plan on page 71.)

**Key Question**

- Which collaboration structures will support the professional learning needed to achieve our goals? (Shared Classroom Experiences, Mathematics Content Learning Team, Mathematics Vertical Learning Team)

**SMART Goals**

SMART goals (Conzemius and Morganti-Fisher 2012) have the following characteristics:

**S**pecific: Includes detailed descriptions of what the goal is; where, when, and how often it will be addressed; and who will be involved

**M**easurable: Identifies what will be seen, heard, and felt when the goal is reached

**A**ttainable: Refers to the level of confidence that the goal can be achieved

**R**elevant: Identifies the objective and purpose for the goal

**T**imely: Includes deadlines that are flexible and realistic

Strategic Planning Sessions

# Action Plan

1.  What is your story to tell in May or June?

    This Is Happening Inside the Classroom . . .   Every day, students will be engaged in rich math tasks that allows them to develop understanding of Standards' core content through mathematical practices. The teacher poses interesting and challenging questions, while the students are highly engaged in solving problems.

    This Is Happening Outside the Classroom . . .   Every teacher will be engaged in collaborative structures for job-embedded professional learning; that includes a Shared Classroom Experience (SCE) working alone or with a peer, instructional coaching, and a Mathematics Content Learning Team (MCLT) at their grade level. One teacher from each grade level will participate on a Mathematics Vertical Learning Team (MVLT).

2.  What actions will be taken to tell the story? What evidence will be collected?

| Inside the Classroom | Evidence |
|---|---|
| Students will be highly engaged in rich math tasks. | Picture of task |
| Teacher will pose challenging questions. | A tally number of questions asked |
| Students will share thinking with other students. | Anecdotal evidence of students' words. |

| Outside the Classroom | Evidence |
|---|---|
| Every teacher will participate in SCE, MCLT, coaching. | Record of participation and reflections. |
| One teacher per grade level will participate in MVLT. | Interim assessments, Common formative assessments. |

For the template used in this Action Plan, see Reproducible 6, Developing an Action Plan, on page 96.

**FIGURE 1–1.  Sample of a District Action Plan**

3. What are the roles and responsibilities of people at your school?
   - Principal effectively messages purpose and focus for math vision, as well as expectations for teacher participation and engagement.
   - Principal creates master schedule for SCE, MCLT, and MVLT meetings, and arranges for substitutes, if necessary.
   - Principal ensures support systems, structures, and processes are in place for teacher learning.
   - Math coach builds coaching relationships with teachers and schedules coaching cycles.
   - All teachers schedule time for SCE and MCLT experiences.
   - One teacher per grade level participates on the MVLT.

4. Which structures for learning will be used and who will participate?

   ✓ Mathematics Content Learning Team

   every teacher will participate to study the math in the upcoming unit

   ✓ Mathematics Vertical Learning Team

   one teacher per grade level

   ✓ Shared Classroom Experience

   every teacher participates either individually or with a peer.

   Instructional Coaching

   each teacher engages in one coaching cycle per month

**FIGURE 1–1. Sample of a District Action Plan** *(continued)*

See Reproducible 6, Developing an Action Plan on page 96.

Now campus teams begin to discuss the nuts and bolts of how to implement the Action Plan. The first step is for all teams to determine the best way to share the Vision Statement (created in Step 1) and Action Plan with their school. Each campus group can dive right in and articulate their school's particular plan, down to scheduling the Mathematics Content Learning Team and Mathematics Vertical Learning Team meetings, and outlining expectations for the Shared Classroom Experiences. Or read what the campus group for Lamar Elementary did (see the "It Really Can Happen" section that follows). It all depends on the size and personality of the schools; administrators must make a judgment call on the best way to complete this step in partnership with individual schools.

## It Really Can Happen . . . Insights from the Field

The principal and math coaches of Lamar Elementary School in Pampa decided to hold their school-level Strategic Planning Session 1 before school started. At the district-level session, they drafted an initial agenda for their school-level session:

- Present the District Vision Statement and Action Plan to the entire faculty, summarizing the process the district team underwent to articulate the vision and goals.

- Describe the collaboration structures that will be used to implement the changes: Mathematics Content Learning Team (Structure 2), Shared Classroom Experience (Structure 3), and Mathematics Vertical Learning Team (Structure 4).

- Assign teachers to small groups by grade level so each grade-level team can discuss what steps will be most useful to take to move toward the Vision Statement.

- Circulate during the discussions to listen to teachers' feedback and share any further details or information to facilitate the process.

- Facilitate each grade-level team's individual Action Plan.

## At the school . . .

After teachers have reviewed the Vision Statement and Current Realities Charts (created in Step 1), they address the Action Plan, either designing their own in alignment with district goals or adapting the initial plan created at the district-level session. If necessary, the facilitator should introduce or review the collaborative structures that will be used to facilitate professional learning (see page 63). When the school's Vision Statement and Action Plan are finalized, teachers collaborate to discuss steps they can take to implement the goals set forth in these documents.

**It Really Can Happen . . . Insights from the Field**

The principal and math coach of Lamar Elementary recreated the entire district-level Strategic Planning Session 1 for their faculty before school started. They had teachers work in grade-level teams to look at their own practices and decide which action steps they could start with in their classroom. All groups were to participate in Mathematics Content Learning Teams by grade level, Mathematics Vertical Learning Teams across grade levels, and Shared Classroom Experiences. Grade-level teams had autonomy in determining topics for study in the Mathematics Content Learning Teams, for choosing the focus of the Mathematics Vertical Learning Teams, and for scheduling productive Shared Classroom Experiences. As teachers talked, the principal and math coach listened to their conversations and noted questions and issues that arose. They used this information to help guide the discussions during the Mathematics Content Learning Team activities.

**Your Turn**

While thinking about how a Strategic Planning Session would support your school, consider the following questions:

- What structures are currently in place on your campus to support student achievement?
- How are you ensuring math achievement is not compromised?
- What actions are working to support student achievement? How do you know?
- What is one step you could take now to support student achievement?

**Key Questions**

- What roles and responsibilities do teachers, teacher leaders, math coaches, and principals need to take on to implement the Action Plan?
- What should be scheduled on the calendar for the school year?
- What evidence should be collected to assess impact?

## Step 3: Who Will Do What and When, and How Will We Assess the Impact? (45–60 minutes)

### At the district . . .

*Objective: Specify who will implement the actions; include calendaring* (**Roles and Responsibilities Chart, Calendar**)

First, the group as a whole discusses the roles of district administrators, curriculum directors, principals, math coaches, and teachers in terms of how to accomplish the actions in the District Action Plan. For example, if one action is to *Ensure support systems and structures are in place* (refer back to Figure 1–1 for a sample District Action Plan) so that professional learning can occur at the building level, the group may decide the assistant superintendent and the director of elementary curriculum will be responsible for checking in with principals and math coaches at each school to ensure they have the resources and plans in place for the necessary meetings to happen. The whole group creates a Roles and Responsibilities Chart, designating who is responsible for implementing each action in the District Action Plan. This can be a separate chart or integrated in the Action Plan. In addition, teams discuss how to assess whether an action has been successful, determining which criteria should be met. Using our sample action—*Ensure support systems and structures are in place*—data can be collected that show the name of the structure (such as Mathematics Content Learning Team or Mathematics Vertical Learning Team), how often the teams meet, how learning is recorded, how learning is facilitated, and how changes are documented.

Each campus group now considers the roles and responsibilities each person will take to implement their particular plan. For instance, if a group decides there will be a Mathematics Content Learning Team, they may designate the math coach to be the point person and determine she is responsible for scheduling the meetings, distributing resource materials, and facilitating the first meeting. The campus group may call on the district math coordinator to assume responsibility for finding relevant resource materials and sharing them with the math coach. Each campus group creates its own Roles and Responsibilities Chart, summarizing what each person will do for each step. This chart should be posted at the corresponding elementary school in a place that is visible to the people responsible.

Participants also revisit the dates set for the next two district-level Strategic Planning Sessions. Then, campus groups revisit the dates set for the three school-level Strategic Planning Sessions. Changes to dates are made as necessary to accommodate everyone's schedules.

## At the school . . .

Campus representatives (the key math coach and teacher who attended the district-level session) share the Roles and Responsibilities Chart created at the district-level session so there is transparency about the process. The Math Leadership Team might want to create their own school Roles and Responsibilities Chart and define the structures they need and how the coach, principal, and district administrators will support them in implementing new practices, such as Mathematics Content Learning Teams or Shared Classroom Experiences.

After the Math Leadership Team has created their Action Plan (see Step 2) and clarified everyone's roles and responsibilities, it is important to create a Calendar to identify when actions will happen. In Pampa, schools simply used a school calendar to highlight dates for the next two Strategic Planning Sessions, the Mathematics Content Learning Team Meetings (Structure 2), Mathematics Vertical Learning Team Meetings (Structure 4), and Shared Classroom Experience (Structure 3). Because Mondays had been designated as professional learning days, learning team meetings were scheduled on those days (see Figure 1–2 for a sample of a Calendar).

Color coding creates an easy, convenient visual means for making the learning real and doable. In Figure 1–2, the three Strategic Planning Sessions are highlighted in red (circles), the seven Mathematics Content Learning Team meetings are highlighted in purple (squares), the seven Mathematics Vertical Learning Team meetings are highlighted in green (triangles), and the four Shared Classroom Experiences are highlighted in blue (rectangles).

By the end of Step 3, everyone should be clear on their role in implementing the Action Plan and know when professional learning activities will occur.

For tips on clarifying roles throughout the school year, see page 87.

# Lamar Elementary School

## July

| S | M | T | W | T | F | S |
|---|---|---|---|---|---|---|
|   |   |   |   |   | 1 | 2 |
| 3 | 4 | 5 | 6 | 7 | 8 | 9 |
| 10 | 11 | 12 | 13 | 14 | 15 | 16 |
| 17 | 18 | 19 | 20 | 21 | 22 | 23 |
| 24 | 25 | 26 | 27 | 28 | 29 | 30 |
| 31 |   |   |   |   |   |   |

## August

| S | M | T | W | T | F | S |
|---|---|---|---|---|---|---|
|   | 1 | 2 | 3 | 4 | 5 | 6 |
| 7 | 8 | 9 | 10 | 11 | 12 | 13 |
| 14 | 15 | 16 | 17 | 18 | 19 | 20 |
| 21 | 22 | {(23 | 24 | 25 | 26 | 27 |
| 28 | 29 | 30 | 31 |   |   |   |

## September

| S | M | T | W | T | F | S |
|---|---|---|---|---|---|---|
|   |   |   |   | 1 | 2 | 3 |
| 4 | 5 | 6 | 7 | 8 | 9 | 10 |
| 11 | 12 | 13 | 14 | 15 | 16 | 17 |
| 18 | 19 | 20 | 21 | 22 | 23 | 24 |
| 25 | 26 | 27 | 28 | 29 | 30) |   |

## October

| S | M | T | W | T | F | S |
|---|---|---|---|---|---|---|
|   |   |   |   |   |   | 1 |
| 2 | (3 | 4 | 5 | 6 | 7 | 8 |
| 9 | 10 | 11 | 12 | 13 | 14 | 15 |
| 16 | 17 | 18 | 19 | 20 | 21 | 22 |
| 23 | 24 | 25 | 26 | 27 | 28 | 29 |
| 30 | 31 |   |   |   |   |   |

## November

| S | M | T | W | T | F | S |
|---|---|---|---|---|---|---|
|   |   | 1 | 2 | 3 | 4) | 5 |
| 6 | (7 | 8 | 9 | 10 | 11 | 12 |
| 13 | 14 | 15 | 16 | 17 | 18 | 19 |
| 20 | 21 | 22 | 23 | 24 | 25 | 26 |
| 27 | 28 | 29 | 30 |   |   |   |

## December

| S | M | T | W | T | F | S |
|---|---|---|---|---|---|---|
|   |   |   |   | 1 | 2 | 3 |
| 4 | 5 | 6 | 7 | 8 | 9 | 10 |
| 11 | 12 | 13 | 14 | 15 | 16 | 17 |
| 18 | 19 | 20 | 21 | 22 | 23 | 24 |
| 25 | 26 | 27 | 28 | 29 | 30 | 31 |

## January

| S | M | T | W | T | F | S |
|---|---|---|---|---|---|---|
| 1 | 2 | 3 | {(4 | 5 | 6 | 7 |
| 8 | 9 | 10 | 11 | 12 | 13 | 14 |
| 15 | 16 | 17 | 18 | 19 | 20 | 21 |
| 22 | 23 | 24 | 25 | 26 | 27 | 28 |
| 29 | 30 | 31 |   |   |   |   |

## February

| S | M | T | W | T | F | S |
|---|---|---|---|---|---|---|
|   |   |   | 1 | 2 | 3 | 4 |
| 5 | 6 | 7 | 8 | 9 | 10 | 11 |
| 12 | 13 | 14 | 15 | 16 | 17) | 18 |
| 19 | 20 | (21 | 22 | 23 | 24 | 25 |
| 26 | 27 | 28 | 29 |   |   |   |

## March

| S | M | T | W | T | F | S |
|---|---|---|---|---|---|---|
|   |   |   |   | 1 | 2 | 3 |
| 4 | 5 | 6 | 7 | 8 | 9 | 10 |
| 11 | 12 | 13 | 14 | 15 | 16 | 17 |
| 18 | 19 | 20 | 21 | 22 | 23 | 24 |
| 25 | 26 | 27 | 28 | 29 | 30 | 31 |

## April

| S | M | T | W | T | F | S |
|---|---|---|---|---|---|---|
| 1 | 2 | 3 | 4 | 5 | 6 | 7 |
| 8 | 9 | 10 | 11 | 12 | 13) | 14 |
| 15 | 16 | 17 | 18 | 19 | 20 | 21 |
| 22 | 23 | 24 | 25 | 26 | 27 | 28 |
| 29 | 30 |   |   |   |   |   |

## May

| S | M | T | W | T | F | S |
|---|---|---|---|---|---|---|
|   | 1 | 2 | 3 | 4 | 5 |
| 6 | 7 | 8 | 9 | 10 | 11 | 12 |
| 13 | 14 | 15 | 16 | 17 | 18 | 19 |
| 20 | 21 | 22 | 23 | 24 | 25 | 26 |
| 27 | 28 | 29 | 30 | 31 |   |   |

## June

| S | M | T | W | T | F | S |
|---|---|---|---|---|---|---|
|   |   |   |   |   | 1)} | 2 |
| 3 | 4 | 5 | 6 | 7 | 8 | 9 |
| 10 | 11 | 12 | 13 | 14 | 15 | 16 |
| 17 | 18 | 19 | 20 | 21 | 22 | 23 |
| 24 | 25 | 26 | 27 | 28 | 29 | 30 |

## Legend

- ○ Strategic Planning
- □ Content Learning Teams
- △ Vertical Learning Teams
- ⌐ ¬ Shared Classroom Experiences

| REPORTING PERIODS | DAYS |
|---|---|
| FIRST SIX WEEKS | 28 |
| SECOND SIX WEEKS | 24 |
| THIRD SIX WEEKS | 30 |
| FOURTH SIX WEEKS | 33 |
| FIFTH SIX WEEKS | 32 |
| SIXTH SIX WEEKS | 32 |
| **TOTAL SCHOOL DAYS** | **179** |
| **Preparation/Inservice** | **8** |
| **Total Days** | **187** |

- Testing Days
- Holidays
- Snow Days
- Prep. Day*/ Inservice
- Early Release Day
- Summer In-service

( BEGIN SIX WEEKS
) END SIX WEEKS
{ BEGIN SEMESTER
} END SEMESTER

**SNOW / MAKE-UP DAYS**
April 9
April 30

FIGURE 1–2. **Sample of a Calendar**

Session 1 Creating a Shared Vision and Making an Action Plan

**It Really Can Happen . . .
Insights from the Field**

As part of the first Strategic Planning Session of the school year in August, faculty at four elementary schools created visuals on chart paper of what all math classrooms should like and sound like (see the photo of one of these visuals). This activity helped each campus group think about and create a VIsion Statement as well as action plans (see the photo of one of the school's plans here). Then the campus groups combined their action plans and selected three actions to form their district-level Action Plan.

For a Vision Statement and Action Plan to happen, each school professional agreed to do the following on a Roles and Responsibilities Chart:

*Math Coaches:*  Engage in Shared Classroom Experiences, practice with teachers, deepen knowledge of math content and processes, identify formative assessment strategies, create a culture of collaboration, document student thinking, reflect on supports for students

*Teacher:*  Design lessons with math coach, participate in Shared Classroom Experiences and learning teams, use formative assessment strategies, redesign lessons to support students

*Principal:*  Communicate expectations clearly, schedule time for teacher collaboration, participate in Shared Classroom Experiences, and monitor and reflect on progress

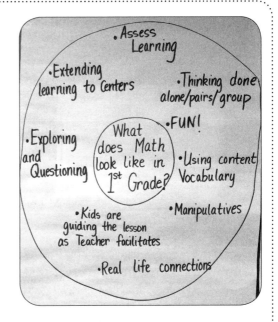

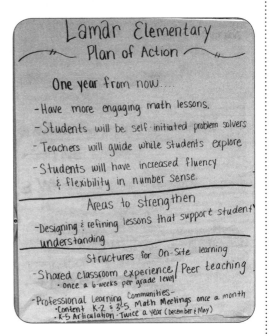

## The Framework for Strategic Planning Session 1

### Before the district-level session, the initiator

1. *Meets for approximately 30 minutes with key leaders to define the purpose of Strategic Planning Sessions and determine who should attend.* The initiator asks the following questions:
   - What changes do we envision in mathematics instruction?
   - What are Strategic Planning Sessions and how will they help make these changes a reality?
   - Who should be present and why?
   - When can we meet?

2. *Schedules Strategic Planning Sessions.* First the three district-level sessions are scheduled. Then the school-level sessions are calendared (three sessions for each school). For Strategic Planning Session 1, the school-level session should happen within two weeks after the district-level session. For Strategic Planning Sessions 2 and 3, the school-level sessions should happen within two weeks before the district-level sessions.

3. *Prepares materials for Session 1.* The initiator prepares necessary materials, including an agenda (Reproducible 2, Strategic Planning Session 1 Agenda [Key Questions]); chart paper or technology with which to create the Vision Statement (Reproducible 5, Developing a Vision Statement), Current Realities Chart, Action Plan (Reproducible 6, Developing an Action Plan), and Roles and Responsibilities Chart; the district calendar; and any data that could inform the discussion.

   *See Reproducibles 2, 5, and 6 on pages 92, 95, and 96.*

### During the district-level session, the facilitator

4. *Establishes norms for productive collaborative discussion.* The facilitator begins a discussion about the shared purpose, namely to improve math achievement by building teacher knowledge. To ensure a safe, collaborative atmosphere that supports inquiry, team members must agree to follow certain norms during meeting, such as the Seven Norms of Collaboration (see page 59).

5. *Guides participants to create a vision of what math instruction should look like ideally in the district.* Together or in campus groups, participants describe in detail what an effective math classroom looks like and create a Vision Statement to summarize the components.

6. *Leads a collaborative discussion to determine what steps need to be taken to achieve the vision.* Together or in campus groups, participants create a Current Realities Chart to document the current state of mathematics instruction, then discuss the actions they need take to move toward the vision. The three highest priority items become the Action Plan.

7. *Supports participants as they determine the roles and responsibilities for personnel and commit to professional learning activities.* Both at the district and school-level, participants identify and record who will take on the roles and responsibilities necessary for implementing the Action Plan, creating a Roles and Responsibilities Chart. In addition, participants schedule professional learning activities if possible, and set dates and times for Sessions 2 and 3.

8. *Elicits ideas for assessing actions.* The group discusses which types of data can be used to measure the success of actions, such as classroom walkthrough observations, student benchmark data, math coach observations, video clips showing teachers' practice in action, and teachers' documentation of intentional changes they have made to practice.

### After the district-level session, the initiator

9. *Confirms that the Action Plan is communicated to each school and that each school has the support it needs to implement it.* Each school holds its own school-level Strategic Planning Session 1 to share information from the district meeting and to develop a customized Action Plan for the school.

10. *Prepares for Strategic Planning Session 2* (see Reproducible 3, Strategic Planning Session 2 Agenda [Key Questions] on page 93).

 **Comparing a Strategic Planning Session with Other Meetings**

Often, teachers, teacher leaders, math coaches, and principals work in isolation or hierarchical groups, seeing others only in passing. Do any of these meetings happen in your school?

- Principals attend a weekly district meeting with district-level administrators.
- Teachers attend weekly team meetings with a math coach or teacher leader.
- The principal conducts monthly staff meetings.

Compare these meetings with a Strategic Planning Session. What is similar? Different?

Rarely do educators meet within the school as "close to the classroom as possible" and collaborate together about "problems of practice," or examine beliefs related to teaching and learning. During a Strategic Planning Session, the invisible wall separating principal, teacher, coach, and/or teacher leader is removed. The session brings them together, encouraging conversations and the sharing of the same goals.

## Session 2  Assessing Impact and Addressing Challenges

**Approximate Time**  District level: 2–3 hours; School level: 1 hour

**Scheduling**  This session occurs midway through the school year, typically in December or January. The school-level session occurs within two weeks before the district-level session so schools can share their progress with the district.

See
Reproducible 3,
Strategic Planning
Session 2 Agenda
(Key Questions), on
page 93.

### Objectives

- Assess progress, documenting and celebrating successes.
- Assess progress, documenting and considering challenges.
- Identify next action steps.
- Document the learning.

| Step | Documents to Revisit, Revise, or Create | |
|---|---|---|
| | *School Level* | *District Level* |
| Step 1: What's changed and what is the evidence of that change?<br><br>Step 2: What challenges have we faced and how can we address them?<br><br>Step 3: What are the next steps toward our vision? | Vision Statement: revisit | Vision Statement: revisit |
| | Current Realities Chart: update | Current Realities Chart: update |
| | Action Plan: revise | Action Plan: revise |
| | Roles and Responsibilities Chart: update | Roles and Responsibilities Chart: update |
| Step 3: (listed above) | Professional Learning Record: create | Professional Learning Record: create |

**Key Questions**
- Where did we start?
- Where are we now?
- What is working well?

## Step 1: What's Changed and What Is the Evidence of That Change? (30–45 minutes)

### At the school . . .

*Objective: Assess progress, documenting and celebrating successes*

The documents created during Strategic Planning Session 1 should be posted for all participants to see:

- Vision Statement
- Current Realities Chart
- Action Plan
- Roles and Responsibilities Chart

The facilitator begins with a brief check-in to build rapport, followed by a quick review of the norms of collaboration (see page 58). Then, participants review the documents, remembering where they were when the school year began. Next, participants consider where they are now and update the Current Realities Chart, using a different-color marker or creating a new chart dated midyear. The facilitator prompts participants to note any changes, such as

- Physical environment
- Teacher and student behavior during lessons
- Evidence of student learning
- Use of new instructional practices, such as formative assessments

Other data, such as test scores, teacher observations, student work samples, and anecdotal records, can be presented and discussed at this point.

In addition to the items evidenced in the classroom, participants should consider changes such as

- Professional learning activities
- Level of collaboration among teachers
- Roles of math coach, administrators, and district staff
- The use of new materials and resources

These changes can be noted on the Current Realities Chart as well.

As participants review and discuss the changes that have taken place during the past several months, they take time to consider the successes they have observed. It is important to note and celebrate them, even if they seem small. Change can be incremental, and acknowledging each step toward a goal builds confidence and momentum. For example, if a school's Action Plan included completing two Shared Classroom Experiences per semester, and the planning, teaching, and debriefing for two such sessions occurred, congratulate participants. Invite them to share their experience and discuss the positives, even if not everything went as anticipated. Perhaps the lesson didn't engage students as hoped, or the majority of students needed reteaching; this is valuable information that can inform future instructional decisions. And the relationships built by planning and teaching together can have positive benefits well beyond one Shared Classroom Experience.

## At the district . . .

Each campus group displays its documents from its school-level Strategic Planning Session 2; a representative from each campus group reviews briefly for the whole group where they were at the beginning of the year and what changes have occurred since then. Campus representatives relate the successes achieved at their school, highlighting actions taken as specified on the Action Plan and other activities that have helped the school move toward the vision expressed in the Vision Statement. As representatives share, participants from other schools can ask questions and offer suggestions; this cross-pollination of ideas can help all schools as they work toward their common vision.

**Key Question**

• What is not working as well as we'd like?

## Step 2: What Challenges Have We Faced and How Can We Address Them? (45–75 minutes)

### At the school . . .

*Objective: Assess progress, documenting and considering challenges*

After documenting and celebrating successes, it's time to consider the challenges faced during the past several months. A helpful starting point is to look at the Action Plan and note what challenges there have been in implementing the actions. In addition, participants can consider the Vision Statement and discuss what is preventing them from achieving some of the descriptors. When discussing challenges, it's especially important for the facilitator is to keep participants focused on the goals and not get sidetracked by other issues. Facilitators can help maintain group focus by

- Referring to the agreed-on norms for collaboration from Session 1 (see page 58)
- Stating and/or writing a clear purpose for the outcomes for the session
- Making sure that Step 1 is not overlooked (celebrating successes)
- Reframing challenges as opportunities

For each challenge, participants can brainstorm ideas for solutions. Facilitators may have participants work in pairs, small groups, or a whole group to generate ideas.

### At the district . . .

Campus representatives share the challenges their Math Leadership Teams have identified along with potential solutions they have discussed. Sharing challenges helps educators see that every school has challenges and invites collaboration in addressing them. This is another opportunity for schools to offer ideas and suggestions across campuses.

# Step 3: What Are the Next Steps
## toward Our Vision? (45–60 minutes)

............................
**Key Question**

• What are one to
  three actions we
  can take to move
  toward our vision?

## At the school . . .

*Objective: Identify next action steps and document the learning*
**(Professional Learning Record)**

Addressing challenges in Step 2 helps point out the next steps to take to propel each school forward toward its vision. With the Action Plan and ideas for facing specific challenges fresh in mind, participants should determine one to three concrete steps they can take to address challenges standing in the way of implementing the actions in the Action Plan or achieving the vision. For instance, if teachers had difficulty planning an effective lesson for the Shared Classroom Experience, one action could be to involve the math coach in the planning process next time for extra support. In addition, take time to document in the Professional Learning Record the professional learning that took place since the last meeting.

## At the district . . .

As campus representatives discuss at a district level the challenges they face at their school, issues may arise that are not challenges per se but that need to be addressed with teachers or students. For example, perhaps the math coach has observed teachers are not using formative assessments effectively and believes this deficiency contributed to the mismatch of instruction to student readiness in the Shared Classroom Experience. As campus representatives share their revised Action Plans, they can note such issues and plan to address them through the collaborative structures in place. In our example, the school's Action Plan already calls for the math coach to get involved in the planning stage of the next Shared Classroom Experience, so the coach can make a point to discuss formative assessments then. As this action is shared at the district level, other coaches and administrators may have tips for how to broach the topic or they may have formative assessments they recommend. In addition, take time to document in the Professional Learning Record the professional learning that took place since the last meeting.

*"Any time you're making a change like this, it's way more than one person. It's a team of people who are committed to the vision."*

—Evan Smith, deputy superintendent

## Session 3 — Acknowledging Progress and Planning for Continuous Improvement Steps

**Approximate Time**    District level: 2–3 hours; School level: 1 hour

**Scheduling**    This session occurs at the end of the school year, typically in May. The school-level session happens within two weeks before the district-level session so schools can share their progress with the district.

See Reproducible 4, Strategic Planning Session 3 Agenda (Key Questions) on page 94.

### Objectives

- Assess progress, documenting and celebrating successes.
- Identify and document what's been learned.
- Think ahead to the upcoming school year.

| Step | Documents to Create or Revisit | |
|------|-------------------------------|---|
| | *School Level* | *District Level* |
| Step 1:  What's changed and what is the evidence of that change? | Vision Statement | Vision Statement |
| | Current Realities Chart: update | Current Realities Chart: update |
| | Action Plan: revise | Action Plan: revise |
| Step 2:  What have we learned?<br><br>Step 3:  Where are we going? | Roles and Responsibilities Chart: update | Roles and Responsibilities Chart: update |
| Step 2: (listed above) | Professional Learning Record: update | Professional Learning Record: update |

## Step 1: What's Changed and What Is the Evidence of That Change? (30–60 minutes)

**Key Question**
- What changes have we seen from our progress assessment during Session 2?

### At the school . . .

*Objective: Assess progress, documenting and celebrating successes*

This session opens in much the same way as Step 1 in Session 2. See page 74 for a full description. Participants update the Current Realities Chart to record changes.

### At the district . . .

The district meeting also opens in much the same way as it did for Step 1 in Session 2. See page 75 for a full discussion.

## Step 2: What Have We Learned?

(Approximate Time 45–60 minutes)

**Key Question**
- How can we summarize what we've learned?

### At the school . . .

*Objective: Identify and document what's been learned*

As teachers reflect on the changes that have occurred throughout the year, they document what they learned from their experiences. The facilitator records teacher insights, math strategies, instructional practices, helpful resources, and tips on chart paper or a digital device, if the screen can be displayed. Participants also document ideas that did *not* work, so they can be adapted or replaced instead of repeated. This information should become part of the Professional Learning Record, which is shared with all participants after the meeting so individuals can consult it as they plan ahead for the next year. This record will also be a key document for the school when it meets to develop its Vision Statement and Action Plan the following year.

### At the district . . .

Campus representatives share their learning at the district level, including ideas that were not successful. The facilitator creates a master document of all learning—the Professional Learning Record—to distribute to team members. This sharing is an excellent opportunity to identify strategies, practices, and tools that worked across campuses; it is also helpful for other schools to hear ideas that perhaps they can incorporate the following year. The district-level team can identify what it wants to keep in place for the following year and what improvements are needed.

**Key Question**

• What changes do we want to see at the end of next year?

## Step 3:  Where Are We Going? (45–60 minutes)

### At the school . . .

*Objective:  Think ahead to the upcoming school year*

Participants now look ahead to the next year and ask, "Where are we going?" It is helpful to refer to the current year's Vision Statement and see which areas have been achieved and which ones are still in progress. Participants can create a new Vision Statement to guide their work for the next year, or simply choose areas from the current document to focus on. As appropriate, they can update or create a new Action Plan and/or Current Realities Chart. For example, at its school-level Strategic Planning Session 3, Travis Elementary School added this item to its Vision Statement: *We want to improve teachers' math content knowledge and understanding of how students learn mathematics by increasing the number of Shared Classroom Experiences.* In addition, participants reflect on the process of all of the Strategic Planning Sessions, noting any procedural issues that can be improved going forward.

### At the district . . .

The facilitator asks everyone to explore the question "Where are we going?" Each campus reviews its Vision Statement, Action Plan, and Current Realities Charts, and shares how it envisions mathematics instruction and classrooms will look on its campus one year from now. As a whole, the group considers what will it take to get each school to this vision; campus representatives take notes and amend their documents as necessary. The documents will likely need to be revisited in the fall if there are changes in faculty and administration; however, they provide a starting place for next year so professional learning can get up and running more quickly.

In addition, during the last ten minutes of the session, the facilitator encourages participants to reflect on the experience of participating in all the Strategic Planning Sessions, asking them to consider questions such as: How were the sessions meaningful and valuable learning places? What should we keep doing, start doing, or abandon for the upcoming year's Strategic Planning Sessions?

# Strategies for Success

Planning a series of Strategic Planning Sessions requires an investment in time and resources, but the payoff is significant. We compiled a set of strategies we use to maximize the potential of the sessions.

## Invite Participants Well in Advance

It's crucial to identify how each session's time, date, and purpose will be communicated clearly to all participants. Often, a meeting is scheduled at the district office, and people at school are notified at the last minute. They show up at the meeting frustrated and resentful because they had to leave their classrooms on short notice and scramble for a sub—without really knowing why. To ensure a more positive mindset of participants, we recommend inviting them to the session as soon as it is scheduled and including details about the purpose of the session in the invitation. This accommodation has the added benefit of priming participants to be thinking about their math instruction before the session even begins. (See Figure 1–3 for a sample invitation via email.)

---

**Subject:** District-Level Strategic Planning Session 1

**When:** Thursday, August 6, from 9:00am–12:00pm

**Where:** Lamar Elementary School, Coach's Room

**Purpose:** Create a Vision Statement and Action Plan for improving mathematics teaching and learning

*Please bring the following:*

- Your questions and ideas about what needs to change in classrooms
- Laptop to access data
- School data (math benchmark assessments, math longitudinal state data, classroom observations)

We look forward to learning together about how best to support improvements in mathematics teaching and learning.

---

**FIGURE 1–3. Sample Invitation to a District-Level Strategic Planning Session 1**

## Foster Full Participation

For a Strategic Planning Session to be successful, educators must be able to share their experiences and ideas freely and openly so they create an accurate picture of the current situation, envision common goals, and brainstorm ideas for achieving those goals. Only through true collaboration in which all participants contribute can a team generate plans to achieve a vision that makes a significant impact on student lives. To foster complete participation, facilitators can try these strategies:

1. **Think alone.** Each participant has at least one minute of quiet time to record thoughts and process information.

2. **Talk, then listen.** After thinking alone, participants pair up with another person and share ideas for one minute, then listen for one minute to the other person.

3. **Write to remember.** At any point during or at the end of the session, each participant uses a digital device or designated session journal to record new ways of thinking about a key topic, such as: How can we increase student engagement in math lessons?

4. **Record your thoughts.** This strategy encourages everyone to record their ideas in writing first, which increases the chance people will share their ideas during discussions. Give participants a set of sticky notes. Encourage them to jot down ideas on the notes during the discussion. When appropriate, pause and ask everyone to write an idea in response to a question before beginning a discussion. As you circulate, remind groups to ask members to share their notes so that everyone's ideas are heard. Another way to use sticky notes is to pose a question and ask everyone to write a response on a note and then stick the note on a chart. In this way, every person's response is recorded.

5. **Listen behind the scenes.** If there is a participant (or several participants) who is strongly vocal and may be disruptive, be proactive and ask a key district leader to engage the participant *before* the session. Often, if potentially disruptive or disengaged individuals have someone to listen to them and hear their ideas for three to five minutes prior to the formal session, participation in large group sharing has a better outcome.

6. **Ask to share others' thoughts.** Ask an individual if another individual—say, a colleague or facilitator—would share his or her idea. In this way, those reluctant to share ideas with the whole group can still contribute.

## Rein in Those Who Dominate the Discussion

For participants who dominate or "hold the floor" by talking too long, facilitators can use these strategies:

- **Designate the speaker.** Ask a person who sits in a certain position at the table to speak for the small group, such as, "The person who sits at the right corner will share the group's ideas."

- **Ask for a big idea summary.** Ask the person who talks extensively to summarize the big idea everyone should know. Say something like, "In one sentence, would you please summarize the big idea you wish to convey?"

## Make the Vision as Vivid as Possible

When participants create a vision successfully, they have a picture of the future, which makes it easier to develop plans to achieve the vision. During a Strategic Planning Session, some participants may have challenges envisioning changes. Facilitators can use the following strategies to help participants envision the future and articulate change.

1. **Pictures in Your Mind.** Ask participants to describe the desired change concretely, with as much detail as possible. For example, if participants are envisioning a math lesson, have them consider the following details:

   - Are students talking? Who are they talking to? The teacher? Other students? Or both?

   - Are students using tools and/or drawing models?

   - How are students making sense of the math task? How do they demonstrate perseverance in solving it?

   - Are students working alone or in groups?

   - What is the teacher doing? Telling how? Asking questions?

   A concrete, specific image promotes a mental vision for change based on which actions can now be planned and undertaken.

2. **Inside and Outside the Classroom.** Ask participants to fold a piece of paper in half or use technology to create a space to envision changes inside and outside the classroom. Label one half of the paper Inside Space; label the other half Outside Space. For Inside Space, educators brainstorm and record changes they would like to see in teaching and student learning, such as: *Students use tools and models daily.* For Outside Space, they record changes they envision in the roles and responsibilities of coaches, principals, and teachers outside the classroom, such as: *Teachers meet with the math coach regularly during a Mathematics Vertical Learning Team meeting to understand more fully how math concepts develop over the grades. The principal attends at least one meeting every quarter.*

## Confirm Consensus on Agreements

By agreeing, a person consents to do something that has been created by the group. During a Strategic Planning Session, after an Action Plan is made, each participant needs to agree to two things: (1) the actions are the ones that should be taken and (2) he or she will participate in accomplishing them.

To confirm consensus on the actions specified in the Action Plan, the facilitator should read each action aloud and ask for participants to signal their consensus, perhaps by putting their thumbs up to indicate agreement or their thumbs down to show dissent. If there is not full agreement, the facilitator should identify the problematic issues, and the group can adjust the action so everyone can agree to it or persuade dissenters to give the action a chance, keeping in mind that the group will reconvene to evaluate progress in a few months. When everyone reaches consensus, the facilitator should ask, "In what situations can the agreements be broken?" People then have an opportunity to state specific situations, such as an emergency in the family or illness (but not a hair appointment!).

**Video Clip 1.1**

### A Strategic Planning Session in Action, Revisited

Revisit the clip you watched earlier in this chapter. As you watch this clip now, identify and talk about what you see happening with regard to each of the following:

- Sharing
- Envisioning
- Goals
- Agreements
- Commitment

See the authors' reflections on these questions in the Appendix.

To view this video clip, scan the QR code or access via mathsolutions.com/GMF11

## Establish a Collaborative Culture through Distributed Leadership

A successful Strategic Planning Session provides space for professionals in various roles to collaborate in pursuit of a common purpose. In order for professionals with different roles to work together, it's necessary to explore how the power dynamic works. If the system is hierarchical, the principal's role is perceived as the authority, then following in succession are math coaches, teacher leaders, and teachers. This structure can make it difficult for some professionals to express their ideas, especially if the ideas are perceived as contrary to those of someone at the top of hierarchy. However, if a school has distributed leadership, everyone is considered a leader—a learner striving for improvement.

Collaborative cultures are ones in which the power dynamic shifts from hierarchical to distributed leadership. In this culture, every professional can influence change. Wise administrators know they do not have as much power to initiate change in instruction as teachers do, so they talk

*"Collaborative cultures are ones in which the power dynamic shifts from hierarchical to distributed leadership. In this culture, every professional can influence change."*

85

with teachers about what's going on in the classroom, gaining information as they build relationships. Ongoing communication focused on student learning creates trust and fosters an environment in which all educators have a shared moral responsibility and purpose for increasing student achievement. With a collaborative culture in place, a Strategic Planning Session becomes a powerful venue for administrators, coaches, and teachers to work together for change.

To ensure a collaborative culture, facilitators must always keep "system oneness" in mind—meaning, during a Strategic Planning Session, for example—people at all levels of a school system (teachers, principals, math coaches, teacher leaders) sit at the same table in the same pursuit of learning. They are given the same professional research and literature to read, and they interact with each other using professional dialogue.

▶ **Video Clip 1.1**

To view this video clip, scan the QR code or access via mathsolutions.com/GMF11

### A Strategic Planning Session in Action, Revisited Again

Rewatch this clip and identify and talk about what you see happening with regard to a collaborative culture. Consider the following questions:

- Is there an obvious leader in each group?
- Can you identify the principals, teachers, or coaches?
- How are educators talking with each other? Does there seem to be an equal amount of listening and talking? Or does one person seem to dominate the conversation?

See the authors' reflections on these questions in the Appendix.

## Research Says . . .

Collaboration, when used effectively, has proved itself to be a useful practice to improve instruction and student achievement (Dumas 2010, Darling-Hammond et al. 2009).

Creating a collaborative school culture is a primary way to improve student achievement (McLaughlin and Talbert 2006, DuFour et al. 2005).

Teachers, principals, and math coaches rarely meet in the same professional places, speak to each other about shared experiences, and/or interact with each other about shared goals (Mullen and Hutinger 2008, McLaughlin and Talbert 2006). In fact, meaningful professional dialogue, focused on improving student learning, is minimal in most schools (Schmoker 2006).

For changes to occur in teachers' practice, educators need opportunities to focus on student learning located within the school, as close to the classroom as possible (Elmore 2002).

## Clarify Roles

Principals, teachers, math coaches, and teacher leaders have multifaceted roles on a campus. Often, roles assigned with good intentions early during the school year lose focus by October amid the hectic school pace. The purpose of the Roles and Responsibilities Chart is to make what each educator does in support of the Action Plan transparent and apparent. We recommend placing this chart in a prominent place at the school, as a visible reminder to all participants. If something is not done, the chart shows whose responsibility it was. If someone is having trouble meeting their responsibilities, a collaborative culture allows the individual to ask for support; it also encourages other educators to offer assistance when they notice a problem. This conversation may take place during a Ten-Minute Meeting (see Chapter 5) or during a Mathematics Content Learning Team meeting (see Chapter 2) or a Mathematics Vertical Learning Team meeting (see Chapter 4). If a teacher is not fulfilling his or her responsibilities, then it is the principal's role to intervene, not the team's or the coach's.

Educators who use Strategic Planning Sessions say the sessions are of crucial importance to the success of an initiative or change. At the end of one of our first Strategic Planning Sessions, we received the following comments:

The principal at Travis Elementary, Ms. Faubion, remarked, "We have to find a way to share this with the entire campus, not just the teachers present."

Ms. Cory, the math coach at Lamar Elementary, expressed, "I feel like it is so much easier to support teachers when we all have a focused vision that a collaborative team identified."

And Ms. Lance, first-grade teacher, confirmed, "Having a plan and vision that is focused on *our* student needs, not one that is given to us from outsiders, makes much more sense."

**Your Turn**  **Design Your Own Strategic Planning Session**

Reproducibles are available for download from mathsolutions.com/ givemefivereproducibles.

Use Reproducible 1, Ten-Step Guide to Strategic Planning Sessions, to plan your own first Strategic Planning Session. Reproducibles for developing the Vision Statement and Action Plan, and facilitating Strategic Planning Sessions 1, 2, and 3 are included at the end of the chapter.

*What has to happen in education today is the focus has to be on student learning. And the focus has to be on teachers gaining the skills, strategies, and knowledge to meet the needs of a very, very diverse population.*

—Evan Smith, deputy superintendent

# Ten-Step Guide to
# Strategic Planning Sessions

### Steps 1–3:  Scheduling the Sessions
### (Purposes, Participants, and Dates)

Hold a thirty-minute meeting with key leaders (representatives of the central office, math coaches, and principals) to discuss the purpose of Strategic Planning Sessions, determine the participants, and calender each one.

1. **Purposes**

   Session 1: _____

   Session 2: _____

   Session 3: _____

2. **Participants**

   District Level: _____

   _____

   _____

   _____

   School Level: _____

   _____

   _____

   _____

3. **Dates**

   Calendar sessions in the following order; school-level sessions are per school.

   District-Level Strategic Planning Session 1 (2–3 hours):

   Date: _____    Time: _____    Location: _____

*(continued)*

School-Level Strategic Planning Session 1 (1 hour, within two weeks after district-level session):

Date: _____    Time: _____    Location: _____

School-Level Strategic Planning Session 2 (1 hour, within two weeks before district-level session):

Date: _____    Time: _____    Location: _____

District-Level Strategic Planning Session 2 (2–3 hours):

Date: _____    Time: _____    Location: _____

School-Level Strategic Planning Session 3 (1 hour, within two weeks before district-level session):

Date: _____    Time: _____    Location: _____

District-Level Strategic Planning Session 3 (2–3 hours):

Date: _____    Time: _____    Location: _____

How is the session information shared with the participants? (email?)

### Step 4:  Planning the Session (What will the session look like?)

4. **Design**

   Design a session with clear outcome and plan for facilitation.

   Begin with the end in mind.

   What are the learning targets? _____

   What will people leave with? (Story to Tell—beginning vision, areas to strengthen, actions to take, plan to share with others)

## Steps 5–10: Facilitating the Session (Key Questions)

*Note that the steps listed here are specific to Strategic Planning Session 1; modify them accordingly for sessions 2–3.*

5. **Vision Statement**

   What story do you want to tell one year from now?

   Write what you imagine: _____

   Think alone; think with team, document story.

6. **Current Realities Chart**

   What data sources will be used to identify strengths and areas to strengthen?

   What are the focus areas to continue strengthening? To start strengthening?

7. **Action Plan**

   What are one to three actions to take to strengthen the focus areas?

   What collaborative structures for learning can be used?

8. **Roles and Responsibilities Chart**

   What will people in each role do?

   When will the plan be shared with others and to their input?

9. **Calendar**

   Which collaborative structures for learning will be used for ongoing professional learning?

   What will the calendar look like?

10. **Progress Assessment**

    What data sources will be used to measure impact?

# Strategic Planning Session 1 Agenda (Key Questions)

1. **Introductions:** Who's in the room? How is everyone? (5 minutes)
   - Make human connections to build rapport.

2. **Norms:** What norms will help us learn together? (5 minutes)

3. **Vision Statement**: Where are we going? (30 minutes)
   - What story is to be told—inside and outside the classroom—at the end of the year?

4. **Current Realities Chart:** What is happening in math classrooms at present? (10 minutes)
   - What are the areas to strengthen?

5. **Action Plan:** What will we do to get there? (20 minutes)
   - What are one to three actions to be taken?

6. **Roles and Responsibilites Chart:** Who will do what? (15 minutes)
   - What actions do principal, teachers, teacher leaders, and math coaches need to take to tell the story?

7. **Calendar:** Which structures will support professional learning—Shared Classroom Experience, Mathematics Content Learning Team, and Mathematics Vertical Learning Team? (15 minutes)
   - When do we have time?
   - What goes on the calendar for the school year?

8. **Progress Assessment:** How will we know if the actions are successful? (15 minutes)
   - What will be measured?
   - What data sources will be used?
   - How will student voice be used in the story?

9. **Looking Ahead:** What are our next steps? Next meeting date? (5 minutes)

# Strategic Planning Session 2 Agenda (Key Questions)

1. **Introduction:** Who's in the room? How is everyone? (5 minutes)
   - Make human connections to build rapport.

2. **Assess Progress:** Where did we start and where are we now? (30 minutes)
   - Revisit the Vision Statement, Action Plan, Roles and Responsibilities Chart. Update the Current Realities Chart.
   - What actions were taken?
   - What are the results?
   - What's working? What's not working?
   - What are we learning about students? About ourselves both personally and professionally?

3. **Next Steps:** Where are we going? (20 minutes)
   - What are solutions to address unique challenges?
   - What is the next action(s) to take?
   - What changes will be made?
   - What did we learn?

4. **Looking Ahead:** What are the next steps and next meeting date? (5 minutes)

# Strategic Planning Session 3 Agenda (Key Questions)

1. **Introduction:** Who's in the room? How is everyone? (5 minutes)
   - Make human connections to build rapport.

2. **Assess Progress:** What is your story to tell? (30 minutes)
   - Share stories. Celebrate!

3. **Assess Progress:** Where have we been? What have we learned? (20 minutes)
   - What actions have been taken and what's been learned from Strategic Planning Sessions 1 and 2?

4. **Assess Progress:** What's working? What's not working? What do we change/not change? (20 minutes)
   - What practices should we keep doing? Stop doing?
   - What practices should we try?

5. **Looking Ahead:** Where are we going? (30 minutes)
   - What will our story be one year from now? Imagine.
   - What are our targets for growth?
   - What professional learning is needed?

6. **Reflection:** What did we learn? How was the process? (15 minutes)
   - Reflect on the Strategic Planning Sessions—both process and content—as a professional learning space.

# Developing a Vision Statement

1. Ask whole school staff: *What do you believe should be in every classroom every day to support students' mathematics learning?*

   - Each person writes one practice on a sticky note (student engagement, modeling, student discourse, formative assessment, etc.).

   - Small table groups cluster practices into themes and categories.

   - Each table identifies and reaches consensus on three practices.

   - Each group writes their three practices on a large piece of chart paper.

   - Whole school staff reaches consensus on three practices by putting sticky dots on their top three choices.

2. How do you know that these practices will support student mastery of mathematics standards? Are your beliefs a match with research?

   - Staff reviews their state's teacher evaluation standards to determine if the three practices they chose will result in student mastery of mathematics standards, or they can look at the three findings from "How People Learn Mathematics" (National Research Council 2005).

# Developing an Action Plan

1. What will be your story to tell in May or June?

   This Is Happening Inside the Classroom . . .

   _____

   _____

   _____

   _____

   _____

   This Is Happening Outside the Classroom . . .

   _____

   _____

   _____

   _____

   _____

2. What actions will be taken to tell the story? What evidence will be collected?

   Inside the Classroom        Evidence

   1. _____    _____

   2. _____    _____

   3. _____    _____

   Outside the Classroom     Evidence

   1. _____    _____

   2. _____    _____

   3. _____    _____

3. What are the roles and responsibilities of people at your school?

_____

_____

_____

_____

4. Which structures for learning will be used and who will participate?

Mathematics Content Learning Team

_____

_____

_____

_____

Mathematics Vertical Learning Team

_____

_____

_____

_____

Shared Classroom Experience

_____

_____

_____

_____

# Tips for Successful Facilitation

- Start with people. Take a few moments to greet everyone and allow time to build relationships.

- Use norms for learning and behaving to keep the team working smoothly.

- Make the purpose clear. Ask, why are people here?

- See the end. Know where the group will be going. Ask, where do you want to end up at the end of the session?

- Design an agenda for learning. Keep the focus on inquiry.

- Anticipate people's entry points. Could they dominate? Do they have an agenda? Is this their first time?

- Voice and choice. Everyone counts and gets at least two options.

- Connect ideas to each other and to practice.

- Consider past, present, and future as a way of building on learning; use this thinking to imagine the future.

- Document learning. What was learned?

- Document next steps. What to do now?

# Tips for Successful Collaboration

### Leveling the Talking Field: Strategies for Getting Educators at Different Status Levels to Talk Together

- Keep the focus on student learning.

- Revisit the focus or vision to remind everyone of the common purpose.

- Remember that everyone in the group has strengths.

- Having different strengths makes a group stronger.

- Foster powerful conversations in which no one dominates.

- Remind administrators that they do not have as much power to initiate change in the classroom as a teacher does.

- Prevent evaluative statements about other professionals from being made.

- It takes time for trust and relationships to be built; it does not happen in one meeting but you can destroy it in one meeting.

- Remember the focus—student learning!

# Chapter 2

# Mathematics Content Learning Team

Research tells us there is a correlation between the level of a teacher's math content knowledge and student achievement (Hill and Ball 2004); the greater a teacher's content knowledge, the higher the student achievement. How can teachers, math coaches, and teacher leaders on the same campus learn together in teams to deepen their understanding of mathematics content for supporting student achievement in mathematics? It's possible with a Mathematics Content Learning Team. This collaboration structure provides time for educators to slow down, communicate, and collaborate as they focus on the mathematics they need to know for teaching and analyze how students understand the math.

In this chapter, we discuss how such a team is designed for learning and taking action. We

- Offer video clips of a team at work
- Provide step-by-step guidelines for facilitating the meetings
- Share tools: Reproducibles for agendas and for planning the meetings
- Suggest strategies for ensuring successful meetings
- Describe variations to meet different needs

We end the chapter with a "Your Turn" that gives you an opportunity to design your own Mathematics Content Learning Team Meeting at the school level.

## Overview

## Tools You Can Use

Videos can be streamed by registering this product at mathsolutions.com/myvideos. See page xxiii for more info.

Tools You Can Use (Reproducibles) appear at the end of the chapter and are also available online at mathsolutions.com/givemefivereproducibles.

# How It Looks in Practice

At Lamar Elementary, a first- and a second-grade teacher, a visiting consultant, a math coach, and the campus principal meet during their bimonthly Mathematics Content Learning Team, which has a teacher focus. The team's Learning Agenda on this day is to deepen their understanding of the math involved in solving the *Number Balances* problem.

 **Video Clip 2.1**

To view this video clip, scan the QR code or access via mathsolutions.com/GMF21

### A Mathematics Content Learning Team in Action

As you watch this clip, which features excerpts from a teacher-focused Mathematics Content Learning Team meeting, consider the following questions:

- What stands out for you about the meeting?
- How do you think teachers and students will benefit from the discussion that took place during the meeting?
- Connect this learning experience to ones you've had. How are they similar and different?

See the authors' reflections to these questions in the Appendix. To see an excerpt of the lesson discussed in Video Clip 2.1, view Video Clip 3.2.

**Your Turn** **Defining a Mathematics Content Learning Team**

Think about words that come to mind when you hear the term *Mathematics Content Learning Team*. Words probably depend on your experiences in participating in a mathematics professional learning community. Consider how a Mathematics Content Learning Team could prove useful and productive. List some of the words that come to mind here:

_____

_____

_____

_____

Based on your ideas gleaned from the video, write a definition in your own words of a Mathematics Content Learning Team.

_____

_____

_____

_____

# What Is a Mathematics Content Learning Team?

## The Equation

Content (subject or topic)

+

Learning (gain or acquire knowledge of or skill in something by study or experience)

+

Team (two or more people working together)

=

Mathematics Success

## The Definition

We define a Mathematics Content Learning Team as two or more school-based professionals (e.g., a principal, math coach, first-grade teacher, and second-grade teacher) collaborating together to deepen their understanding of the knowledge and skills necessary for teaching mathematics effectively. When they are together, math talk predominates. Participants discuss math content, referring to textbooks, curriculum materials, state standards, and professional reading to share and build knowledge, clarify understandings, and develop connections between mathematical skills. They may also analyze student work and assessment data, identifying strategies used proficiently, misconceptions, and gaps in understanding. Together, educators determine *what* students need to learn and discuss *how* they can best teach it.

See Reproducible 14, Big Idea Flow on page 128.

### Three Ways to Organize Mathematics Content Learning Teams

**Teacher Focused.** Participants study mathematics content in an upcoming unit, creating a Big Idea Flow—a trajectory of math ideas as they develop over the course of the unit. For example, when fourth-grade teachers planned a two-week unit on multiplication by two-digit numbers, teachers talked about how to begin with arrays and use expanded notation to develop meaning for the operations, then connect arrays and expanded notation to the standard algorithm. After identifying the Big Ideas, teachers solved a problem, then discussed how they anticipated students' thinking and the strategies for solving the problem. The teachers also discussed the level of sophistication of the different strategies they expect to see, and how to select and sequence student thinking during a lesson. Being able to think about the Big Ideas before the lesson helps teachers be able to document and guide students towards deeper, more efficient strategies. Instead of talking about identifying and planning math activities, team members' talk focuses on mathematical ideas.

**Student Focused.** Participants analyze how students learn math. Teachers, teacher leaders, and math coaches bring student work, snippets of student conversation, anecdotes, or other artifacts that illustrate strategies students use to solve problems. Team members attempt to understand the math behind the various strategies, connect it to their standards, identify students' understanding and misconceptions, and consider thoughtfully cognitive supports—such as manipulatives or visual representations—for increasing students' mastery of the standard.

**Teacher and Student Focused.** This type of team is a hybrid. The first meeting is teacher focused; the team studies the mathematics in an upcoming unit of study, as described earlier. The second meeting is student focused; teachers bring student work samples to assess student understanding of the math learning targets of the lessons implemented between the first and second meetings. The result is a cycle of study designed to deepen teachers' math content knowledge and their understanding of students' math thinking and strategies as a result of participating in the lesson.

## Research Says . . .

When schools are engaged in continuous improvement, Learning Forward found that "the community develops collective responsibility for student learning, is results oriented, and community members align adult learning goals with student learning goals" (Hirsh et al. 2014, 227).

Ball and colleagues (2005) remind us that "to implement standards and curriculum effectively, school systems depend upon the work of skilled teachers who understand the subject matter" (14). Mathematics Content Learning Teams effectively develop teachers' knowledge of math content and their skill in teaching it.

Saunders and colleagues (2009, 1011) report that when grade-level teams used a specific protocol with fidelity three hours per month during professional learning meetings, and principals supported and monitored its use, student achievement in mathematics was of statistical and practical significance. To achieve this result, "[g]rade-level teams examined student assessments, set and shared specific academic goals, jointly developed instruction to address these goals, and reviewed student work products," much like is done in a Mathematics Content Learning Team.

# Scheduling Mathematics Content Learning Team Meetings

Mathematics Content Learning Teams, comprised of two or more school-based professionals (e.g., a principal, math coach, first-grade teacher, and second-grade teacher) meet for one hour at least twice a month throughout the school year. The team forms at the beginning of the year, and one of its first tasks is to set dates and times for the entire year's worth of meetings, then enter them on the school calendar.

*"Any time you have an opportunity to collaborate with your peers, you're going to learn something from them. Everyone brings with them different experiences and different ideas. And sometimes we simply need affirmation that we are doing the right things."*

—Andrea Caison, first-grade teacher

While thinking about how a Mathematics Content Learning Team would support your school, consider how teachers at your campus would respond to the following questions:

When we say "students learn math with understanding," we mean . . .

_____

_____

When we say "formative assessment," we mean . . .

_____

_____

When we say "instruction that supports learning," we mean . . .

_____

_____

# What Is the Agenda for the Mathematics Content Learning Team?

The Mathematics Content Learning Team structure provides a time and space for professionals to learn together with a common purpose and focus—to deepen their understanding of mathematics needed for teaching as defined by the standards and to seek insights into strategies students use to learn mathematics. Meeting agendas might look like this:

| Meeting 1:<br>**Launching the Mathematics Content Learning Team** | Meetings 2, 3, and Beyond:<br>**Learning Together in the Mathematics Content Learning Team** |
|---|---|
| Step 1: What is the focus? | Step 1: Are we all connected? |
| Step 2: How do we ensure we stay focused? | Step 2: What math content do we need to learn about more? |
| Step 3: What are our roles and what is the agenda? | Step 3: What have we learned and what are our next steps? |

## Meeting 1 Launching the Mathematics Content Learning Team

**Approximate Time**  60 minutes

**Scheduling**  This meeting happens early during the school year.

**Objectives**

- Establish expectations and set the tone for the year.
- Establish norms and begin team building.
- Set and communicate purpose and goals to participants.
- Clarify roles and responsibilities.
- Create a Learning Agenda to promote discussion and inquiry.

| Step | Documents to Revisit or Create |
|---|---|
| Step 1: What is the focus? | Action Plan: revisit (from Chapter 1) |
| Step 2: How do we ensure we stay focused? | Norms for Behavior and Learning: revisit (from Chapter 1) |
| | Roles and Responsibilities Chart: create |
| Step 3: What are our roles and what is the agenda? | Learning Agenda: create |

## Step 1:  What Is the Focus? (10–20 minutes)

*Objective:  Establish expectations and set the tone for the year*

The first session establishes expectations and sets the tone for the year. The math coach or other math teacher leader facilitates this first session. If the school's Action Plan (refer to Reproducible 6 on page 96) has set a focus for the Mathematics Content Learning Team, the facilitator communicates it to participants. Even if the Action Plan has a focus—say, improving number fluency—it will look different for each grade level. For instance, the kindergarten focus may be on counting and cardinality whereas the fifth-grade focus is on applying and extending previous understandings of multiplication and division. The broad school or district focus must be broken down so that each grade level understands its part and can set its focus accordingly. This is where knowledge of the mathematics learning pathway is important.

**Key Questions**

- What do the data say about our students' mathematical learning needs?
- What is the mathematics content identified by the standards at our grade level?
- What is the learning progression right before and after our grade level?

The math coach can help grade-level teams identify their part in the larger school or district focus, and there are many resources that can be used for this information. If a broad focus has not been set by the school or district, the team can determine its own, based on assessment data and teacher suggestions. Because many elementary teachers spend more time studying the literacy pathway than the math pathway, helping them develop a foundation for mathematics instruction is the power of the content-based learning team.

## Step 2: How Do We Ensure We Stay Focused? (10–20 minutes)

*Objective:  **Establish norms and begin team building***

The designated facilitator establishes norms for group learning using the protocol described in detail in Chapter 1, page 58. See the detailed description of the Seven Norms. A list of norms for behavior and learning to which the group agrees should be documented so it can be referred to at subsequent meetings.

**Key Questions**

- How do we ensure our time together is meaningful, valuable, and relevant to our classroom practice?
- How are we going to ensure we stay focused to learn how to support students?

### Seven Norms of Collaboration

1. Pausing
2. Paraphrasing
3. Putting Inquiry at the Center
4. Probing for Specificity
5. Putting Ideas on the Table
6. Paying Attention to Self and Others
7. Presuming Positive Intentions

*Source:*  Garmston and Wellman (2009) . See Chapter 1 for a full discussion and protocol for introducing norms to learning teams.

## Step 3: What Are Our Roles and What Is the Agenda? (20–30 minutes)

*Objective:  **Clarify roles and responsibilites***

For meetings to run smoothly for groups of more than four people, it is helpful to assign roles so it is clear who is responsible for key tasks. Table 2–1 shows examples of roles that larger teams have used. We highly recommend rotating the roles for each meeting. We learned that when one person, such as the coach, is always the designated facilitator, the group is at a loss when that person is absent. To distribute leadership, promote collaboration, and take ownership of their own professional learning, it helps for team members to rotate all roles, especially the facilitator role. See page 85 for more information on the benefits of distributed leadership.

**Key Questions**

- How can we make our meetings run smoothly?
- How can we structure our meetings to keep focused on math learning?

**TABLE 2–1. Roles and Responsibilities for Mathematics Content Learning Teams of Four or More People**

| Roles | Responsibilities |
|---|---|
| Facilitator | • Prepares the Learning Agenda and emails it at least two days before the meeting, along with reminders about items to bring and actions to take. |
| | • Starts and ends the meeting on time. |
| | • Facilitates team building. |
| | • Guides participants through the Learning Agenda. |
| | • Encourages members to participate. |
| | • Keeps talk focused on mathematics learning, referring to norms as necessary. |
| | • Summarizes the one to three points of learning the group wants to remember and the actions participants will take before the next meeting. |
| Recorder | • Documents the points of learning. |
| | • Documents the actions participants agree to take before the next meeting. |
| | • Reminds participants of the roles they have for the next meeting. |
| | • Emails participants all this information as soon as possible after the meeting. |
| Timekeeper | • Watches the time and cues the facilitator if any step is running longer than planned. |
| | • Alerts the facilitator when there are five minutes left so the team can summarize the learning and plan the actions to take for the next meeting. |
| Team member (everyone at the meeting) | • Comes prepared to the meeting |
| | • Participates actively in the meeting. |
| | • Stays focused on the Learning Agenda. |

*Objective: Create a Learning Agenda to promote discussion and inquiry*

Using an agenda focuses the meeting on a specific topic and provides a structure for the meeting. We call these agendas *Learning Agendas* because acquiring new knowledge and skills in a climate of collaborative inquiry is the focus. Knowledge is to be discovered; therefore, agenda items are more open-ended and call for inquiry and exploration. All too often, agendas for team meetings are used as a "check-off list" so participants can say at the end of the meeting, "We got everything done!" Using a Learning Agenda promotes discussion and inquiry for teams to discover what they don't already know, and also to discover students' math understandings and misconceptions. The team needs to establish a means for creating the agenda for subsequent meetings. Here are three options we have seen teams use with success:

### Ideas for Creating Learning Agendas

1. The team brainstorms a list of topics related to the school's priorities in the Action Plan, displays them for everyone to see, and after discussion votes on a series of topics to be covered over the next several meetings. After that series of meetings is complete, the process is repeated, with the opportunity to add additional topics before deciding on the next series.

2. Each team member submits suggestions to the math coach, and the coach selects one and passes it to the next scheduled facilitator.

3. Alternatively, the facilitator can compile the list and share it with all team members. Then, whoever is serving as facilitator selects the focus from the list.

The option you select depends on the size of your team and member preferences. The key is to have a consistent routine in place that allows all teachers to have a voice; the math coach should not be seen as the "lead facilitator" who sets the agenda of every meeting. Teams are strengthened when all members feel that they have voice and can speak up and state their needs or their students' needs.

Another option for which the team needs to decide is whether the meetings will be teacher focused (studying math content to understand and teach it better) or student focused (analyzing how students learn and think about math concepts). Teams can also choose to alternate between these types of meetings, studying the math content first, then analyzing student thinking about that content next (see page 104 for a more detailed description of these organizational options).

During the initial meeting, create a chart outlining the responsibilities of each role and make a rotation schedule so it's clear who fulfills which role for each meeting. Email the schedule to all participants. In addition, share Reproducible 12, Teacher-Focused Learning Agenda and Reproducible 13, Student-Focused Learning Agenda (located at the end of the chapter), which facilitators use to plan the Learning Agenda for each meeting. Discuss the organization of the agendas (teacher focused, student focused, or both) and how these Learning Agendas can be used to guide meetings.

See Reproducibles 12 and 13 on pages 126 and 127.

## Meeting 2 Learning Together in the Mathematics Content Learning Team

**Approximate Time**    60 minutes

**Scheduling**    Meetings happen biweekly throughout the school year.

**Objectives**

- Create a team-building environment.
- Deepen educators' knowledge of grade-level mathematics concepts.

| Step | Documents to Revisit, Preselect, or Create |
|------|-------------------------------------------|
| Step 1:  Are we all connected? | |
| Step 2:  What math content do we need to learn about more? | Learning Agenda: preselect |
| | Big Idea Flow: create |
| Step 3:  What have we learned and what are our next steps? | Points of Learning: create |
| | Actions: create |

## Step 1:  Are We All Connected? (5 minutes)

*Objective:  Create a team-building environment*

Each meeting should begin with a few minutes of conversation to help team members connect socially and transition from the fast school pace to a slower learning pace, so everyone can be completely and fully present during the learning conversations. If the facilitator thinks it will be helpful, he or she can review or refer briefly to the norms the group agreed on. In addition, this is a great time to celebrate successes; so, inviting participants to share something that worked is a motivating way to begin the meeting. Even small gains being celebrated propel teams forward in bonding and sharing with each other.

**Key Questions**

- What do we need to understand about each other before the meeting starts?
- Is anyone attending who has not attended previously?

*"If I get stuck on something or I need a better way to help the kids understand a certain concept, I have these wonderful people who I can fall back on and use their tools and the resources that they bring."*

—Natalie Davis, fourth-grade teacher

**Key Questions**

• What do students understand about the math content?

## Step 2: What Math Content Do We Need to Learn About More? (50 minutes)

*Objective: Deepen educators' knowledge of grade-level mathematics concepts*

The Learning Agenda is the heart of the meeting and provides a structure for collaborative learning. The agenda differs based on whether the team has a teacher focus or a student focus (see page 104).

See Reproducible 12, Teacher-Focused Learning Agenda, and Reproducible 13, Student-Focused Learning Agenda at the end of the chapter for more. See also Reproducible 15, Tips for a Successful Mathematics Content Learning Team Meeting, at the end of the chapter.

### Sample Teacher-Focused Learning Agenda (50 minutes)

1. *Share actions taken, results, and conclusions about the action.* (10 minutes)  Each person shares the outcome of an action taken after the previous meeting.

2. *What is the focus for learning?* (10 minutes)  What are the math content and practices to be developed in the upcoming unit? How are they connected to our standards?

3. *What is the "Big Idea" Flow in the unit?* (10 minutes)  A "Big Idea" Flow (Reproducible 14) describes the progression of important math concepts throughout a math unit, investigation, or lesson. The flow shows the development of math ideas of concepts and how they build. An effective way to build mathematics knowledge is to chart Big Idea Flows. See the box that follows for a protocol for building a Big Idea Flow.

See Reproducible 14, Big Idea Flow on page 128.

### How to Build a Big Idea Flow

1. Identify the math domain.
2. Identify the math standard(s).
3. Identify the unit.
4. Identify what students are to know and be able to do day-to-day in the unit.
5. Present the math Big Ideas in a representation, diagram, or picture.

**Example**

1. Identify the math domain.
    The math domain in this unit is Number and Operations in Base Ten for third grade.
2. Identify the math standard(s).
    The math standard is: *Use place value understanding and properties of operations to perform multidigit arithmetic.*
3. Identify the unit.
    The math unit is Balancing Number Puzzles.

4. Identify what students are to know and be able to do day-to-day in the unit.

    Students must demonstrate place-value understanding of three-digit numbers using base ten blocks, solve problems using place-value understanding, and add and subtract within 1,000 using strategies and algorithms based on the relationship between addition and subtraction.

5. Present the math Big Ideas in a representation, diagram, or picture.

    A teacher draws a timeline:

    Day 1:  Develop place-value understanding using base ten blocks.

    Day 2:  Solve word problems using place-value understanding.

    Day 3:  Connect place-value models to algorithm, then practice adding and subtracting using algorithms.

    Day 4:  Solidify understanding by practicing solving number puzzle problems.

    Day 5:  Practice understanding using more number puzzles, with an explanation of strategies that show the relationship between addition and subtraction.

6. *What do we need to know about the math content in the upcoming unit?*

    Based on the Big Idea Flow, teachers determine what they need to learn about math content. To guide meaningful conversations about math content, we learned there needs to be a knowledgeable other, such as a math educator or coach, to guide the content conversations. If this is not possible, teachers need to know where to look for the information they need (see "Helpful Resources for Researching Math Content" below).

> For suggestions on planning for unprepared participants and encouraging full participation, see Reproducible 15, Tips for a Successful Mathematics Content Learning Team Meeting on page 129.

## Helpful Resources for Researching Math Content

*Elementary and Middle School Mathematics: Teaching Developmentally* by John Van DeWalle, Karen S. Karp, and Jennifer M. Bay-Williams (2014)

Assists teachers in developing a conceptual understanding of the mathematics they will teach and the most effective methods of teaching Pre-K through 8 math topics. The text uses the Common Core State Standards and National Council of Teachers of Mathematics Principles to Actions, as well as current research with suggestions for how to teach in a problem-based, developmentally appropriate manner that supports the learning needs of all students.

*About Teaching Mathematics: A K–8 Resource, Fourth Edition* by Marilyn Burns (2015)

This resource provides teachers information organized into four parts: Starting Points, which includes issues to address when thinking about teaching mathematics;

Problem-Solving Investigations, which includes lessons, games, and investigations that assist teachers in planning lessons for problem solving; Teaching Arithmetic, which includes ideas for understanding how students learn operations with accompanying assessments; and Questions Teachers Ask, which includes author responses to pedagogical questions from teachers, including authentic problems of practice.

Progressions Documents for the Common Core State Standards for Mathematics by Achieve the Core (2013)

The progressions documents explain why standards are sequenced the way they are, identify cognitive difficulties and pedagogical solutions, and provide more detail on challenging areas of mathematics. Progressions are useful for teachers in organizing curriculum and they provide coherent links between mathematics education research and standards.

**Sample Student-Focused Learning Agenda**

1. *Share actions taken, results, and conclusions about the action.* (10 minutes) Each person shares the outcome of an action taken after the previous meeting.

2. *What's the math problem and how do we understand and solve it?* (10 minutes) Participants discuss a particular type of problem from a unit and share the strategies they use to solve it.

3. *What strategies do students use to solve the problem?* (10 minutes) Participants now analyze examples of student work to determine how students approached the problem. Do they use the same strategies the teachers used? Different strategies? Describe the range of work fully.

4. *What do we need to know about the math behind student strategies?* (10 minutes) What understandings and misconceptions about math do students' strategies reveal? Document them.

5. *What strategies will further students' understanding of the math?* (10 minutes) Participants discuss how to bridge teacher and student understandings of the content, identifying concepts, strategies, and practices that will be helpful for students to learn.

Teams following the hybrid Teacher- and Student-Focused model alternate between the Teacher-Focused Learning Agenda and the Student-Focused Learning Agenda.

See Reproducible 13 (page 127) for a template of this agenda.

## Step 3:  What Have We Learned and What Are Our Next Steps? (5 minutes)

**Key Questions**

- What actions will we take next?
- What evidence will we bring to the next meeting?

Articulate learning points and actions. When there are five minutes left in the meeting, the timekeeper signals the facilitator, who then wraps up the discussion and prompts participants to articulate one to three points of learning they want to remember. The recorder documents these points (Points of Learning) and emails them to participants after the meeting.

Last, the facilitator asks participants to indicate Actions they will commit to doing before the next meeting. We recommend naming one to three actions related to the Learning Agenda; participants begin the next meeting by reporting on the results of those Actions. For the Big Idea Flow described earlier, Actions might be *scaffolding the essential math concepts of place value and not starting with a process or an algorithm, encouraging student use of base ten blocks, fostering student-to-student interactions, and making connections explicit.* The recorder notes these Actions and includes them in the email along with the Points of Learning.

**Video Clip 2.2**

## Building Knowledge in a Mathematics Content Learning Team

In Video Clip 2.1, we see Mathematics Content Learning Team members first solve the *Number Balance* problem themselves and compare their personal solution strategies. They are surprised to learn that, as adults, they all used different strategies. The discussion then leads to the insight that students should be allowed to use the strategy with which they feel most comfortable, as long as it is effective. The teachers then predict the strategies the students would use to solve the *Number Balances* problem and discuss the complexity of the strategies they expect the students to try. They decide to observe closely and note each student's strategy to determine which students need more work with the hundreds chart.

To view this video clip, scan the QR code or access via mathsolutions.com/GMF22

Video Clip 2.2 shows another part of the above meeting. As you watch this clip, consider these questions:

- How did the group respond to the coach's question?
- How did the coach participate?
- What conclusion about student strategy use did teachers reach as a result of the discussion? Do you agree or disagree?

See the authors' reflections on these questions in the Appendix.

> ### It Really Can Happen . . . Insights from the Field
>
> Kindergarten teachers at Midtown Elementary observed students struggling with mastering standards in the Operations and Algebraic Thinking domain—specifically, solving addition and subtraction problems, and adding and subtracting within ten. One teacher, who had been teaching kindergarten for three years remarked, "The kids do fine with addition, but when we get to subtraction, they really struggle. Why is that?" With the help of the math coach, the kindergarten team looked at the pathway to operations, which included identifying six counting skills (rote counting, conservation, one-to-one correspondence, connecting quantity to set, keeping track, and counting by groups) and three relationships on number (anchoring 5 and 10, one-two more and less than; and part–part–whole) that supported students' proficiency with addition and subtraction. The teachers learned there are three levels of counting—counting by ones, counting on, and reasoning—and the goal is for students to leave kindergarten with the most sophisticated level of counting. By identifying the sequence leading to success with operations, the teachers provided students activities to strengthen their counting skills and relationships on number, which resulted in increased scores on the Number and Algebraic Thinking domain.

## The Framework for a Mathematics Content Learning Team

### Before the meeting, the facilitator . . .

1. *Identifies the purpose for learning.* Drawing on the school's Action Plan, assessment data, and/or teacher surveys, the facilitator selects a focused purpose for learning for the next meeting.

2. *Sets the Learning Agenda.* If the learning is teacher focused, such as building mathematics knowledge related to an upcoming unit, then the Teacher-Focused Learning Agenda (Key Questions) (Reproducible 12) can guide the meeting. If the learning is student focused, such as identifying student strengths and challenges and planning instruction to address them, then the Student-Focused Learning Agenda (Key Questions) (Reproducible 13) is used.

3. *Gathers/requests necessary materials.* The facilitator gathers any materials he or she wants to share with the group, such as professional articles or math manipulatives. The facilitator also requests participants bring relevant materials, including curriculum or standards documents and examples of student work.

4. *Determines roles and responsibilities.* Identify who will fulfill which role during the meeting, according to a rotating schedule. Roles include facilitator, recorder, and timekeeper (refer back to Table 2–1); all participants are expected to be active team members.

> For templates of these Agendas, see Reproducibles 12 and 13 at the end of the chapter.

**During the meeting, participants . . .**

5. *Participate in team building.* Spend a few minutes reconnecting with team members and getting in the professional learning mindset. Review norms for learning, if necessary.

6. *Focus the discussion on math, following the appropriate Learning Agenda.* Share the actions and results from last time, then move on to the meeting's current focus for learning.

7. *Document the learning and identify next steps.* Articulate points of learning the group would like to remember; the recorder documents these. Then, identify next steps—the actions each member will take to improve math achievement in his or her classroom; the recorder documents these as well. All notes will be emailed to participants.

**After the meeting, participants . . .**

8. *Take action.* Each participant carries out the action agreed to at the meeting.

9. *Collect and analyze results.* Each participant documents the results of the action, through anecdotal notes or student work, then analyzes the results.

10. *Prepare to share and discuss actions and results at the next meeting.* Each participant prepares a story to tell about the action taken and the results seen.

## Tips for Being Prepared for a Meeting

Email participants two to three days before the meeting with materials requests, a copy of the agenda, and a reminder about to which actions the group agreed at the last meeting. Also include information about who is fulfilling the role of facilitator, recorder, and timekeeper, as these roles alternate.

# Strategies for Success

Mathematics Content Learning Teams can lead to significant growth over the course of a year. Here are some suggestions based on our experience for making this professional learning structure be as effective and efficient as possible.

## Keep Focused on the Agenda

One primary role of the facilitator is to keep the conversations focused on agenda items. Sometimes, a participant interjects a personal concern that takes the conversation in a different direction. We use three strategies to keep focused on the agenda:

1. **Build and Question.** When teachers raise concerns that steer conversation away from the agenda, facilitators can identify the core issues and then frame a question that connects the issues to the agenda item. For example, a teacher said she didn't see why students needed to spend so much time learning different strategies for adding and subtracting because the traditional algorithm works, and learning different strategies takes time. The facilitator responded with three statements that acknowledged her concerns and identified ways the group could build on her ideas:

   Build 1: Learning different strategies takes time.

   Build 2: It is frustrating to watch students struggle with different strategies.

   Build 3: The algorithm we learned was faster and quicker for some of us.

   The facilitator then posed a question to get the discussion back on track: *How can we help students understand why the algorithm works?* This got the conversation back to the agenda item.

2. **Parking Lot with Review.** Sometimes teachers raise important issues that aren't on the agenda but merit full discussion. To handle these types of comments, it's helpful to have a Parking Lot, a place where such ideas are recorded publicly. Issues in the Parking Lot become topics for subsequent meetings. For example, a teacher said her time was being wasted in the Mathematics Content Learning Team because so many of her students were behind. She needed to know what to do with all her kids who couldn't do the grade-level math. The facilitator

acknowledged this was an important idea, but that the topic needed more time to effect a valid discussion. The facilitator put the teacher's issue on a public Parking Lot, noting that differentiation and catch-up strategies would be on the agenda for the next meeting. The group was then able to return to the current meeting's agenda.

3. **The Main Message.** Occasionally, teachers take a long time to express an idea, and it can feel like they are rambling or "holding the floor" with a monologue. To honor the teacher and the group's learning at the same time, the facilitator can interrupt the teacher respectfully with this question: "In one sentence, would you please summarize the main message you wish to convey?" The recorder writes the words and the facilitator gets the team back on track with the agenda conversation.

## Plan for Unprepared Participants

We recommend using a proactive approach to planning for unprepared participants by creating notebooks for everyone that contain all the resources they need for full participation. This strategy prevents participants from missing essential materials, but, occasionally, teachers forget to bring work samples or other items that were agreed to. For example, during one student-focused Mathematics Content Learning Team meeting, a teacher forgot her student work samples, so the facilitator asked her to go back to her room and get them. She then explained that she did not have time to administer the agreed-on assessment from the previous meeting. The grouped moved to problem solving, trying to find ways for her to find time to administer the assessment in the upcoming week. The facilitator stated, "Your students are important to all of us. Let's brainstorm strategies to ensure we get their samples next week." In this way, the group supported the unprepared member and encouraged participants to reach out to one another for help before there were issues that would interfere with the meeting's progress.

## Encourage Full Participation

Each person's voice is important, and the facilitator should state this publicly at the beginning of every meeting. We have used the following strategies to ensure full participation:

- **Play or Pass.** Each person's name is called and he or she can say "Play" and give an opinion, or he or she can say "Pass" because more time is needed to think.

- **Anyone Else?** After a person contributes an opinion or idea, that person asks the group, "Anyone else?" This strategy works best in groups of four or more.
- **Talking Stick.** A talking stick is used to allow one person's voice to be heard at a time. Participants may only speak when they have the stick. This strategy works best in groups of four or more, and when one person dominates the conversation. The stick allows for more people to be heard.

## Probe for Specifics

A typical issue we've noticed in Mathematics Content Learning Team meetings is speaking in generalizations about students. *My kids can't* or *They are so behind* are frequent comments. When this happens, refer to the norm "probe for specificity"; ask questions without sounding like you're interrogating the teacher. It's important to use a tone that sounds genuinely curious, that conveys that you really want to know. For example, *What specifically* can *your students do? What did you hear them say? Is there a work sample from an assessment task we can look at? What is the skill or concept they struggle with?* Remember to pause between each question and listen to what the teacher says, and use an inviting tone, in which the voice goes up at the end of the question.

**Video Clip 2.1**

### A Mathematics Content Learning Team in Action, Revisited

Rewatch Video Clip 2.1 and consider the following questions:

1. How did the facilitator encourage participation?
2. What kinds of specific information were shared? How did these specifics enhance the conversation?

See the authors' reflections on these questions in the Appendix.

To view this video clip, scan the QR code or access via mathsolutions.com/GMF21

## Research Says . . .

In *Transforming Teaching in Math and Science* (Gamoran et al. 2003), the authors point out that when teachers focus on teaching for understanding, they attend to student thinking and focus on powerful mathematical ideas and practices, and equitable classroom learning opportunities. To sustain teaching for understanding, they maintain, teachers must keep learning and growing together professionally. The Math Content Learning Team structure provides time during the school day for teachers, teacher leaders, and math coaches to focus conversations intentionally and deliberately on understanding the quality of mathematics students are learning.

Research helps us understand there is a correlation between teachers using student thinking to guide instruction and student achievement. Student achievement increases when teachers use student thinking to guide instruction (Carpenter et al. 2014). Dylan Wiliam's research (2011) on formative assessment helps us understand how using formative assessment strategies improves student learning. During Mathematics Content Learning Team sessions, professional talk focuses on what students know and can do related to lessons teachers design and implement.

Change and improvement is dependent on learning. A professional learning community is a structure and way of working to provide the environment in which principals and teachers set about learning intentionally to increase their effectiveness and, subsequently, increase positive student results (Hord and Hirsch 2008).

 **Design Your Own Mathematics Content Learning Team Meeting**

Use Reproducible 9, Ten-Step Guide to an Effective Mathematics Content Learning Team Meeting and the Learning Agenda templates (Reproducibles 12 and 13) to design your own Mathematics Content Learning Team Meeting.

# Ten-Step Guide to an Effective Mathematics Content Learning Team Meeting

## Before the Meeting

1. **Purpose:** Identify the purpose using data (understanding math for teaching and/or identifying strategies students use).

2. **Learning Agenda:** Create the agenda.

3. **Resources:** Gather necessary resources (upcoming math unit or problem and/or student work).

4. **Roles and Responsibilities:** Clarify roles and responsibilities (facilitator, timekeeper, recorder, member).

## During the Meeting

5. **Establish Norms:** Set norms for learning and behavior (do this in the very first meeting). For all meetings after the first one, begin with actions taken from the previous meeting.

6. **Content-Specific:** Focus talk on math content.

7. **Learning Points and Actions:** Identify and document learning and action steps.

## After the Meeting

8. **Actions:** Act on next steps.

9. **Evidence:** Document evidence of taking action on next step.

10. **Share:** Identify evidence to take to the next Mathematics Content Learning Team meeting.

# Meeting 1 Agenda
# (Key Questions)

This protocol is designed to be used when any Mathematics Content Learning Team meets for the first time to learn together in a community.

1. **Introduction:** Who's in the room? How is everyone? (5 minutes)

2. **Norms:** What norms will help us learn together? (5 minutes)

3. **Purpose:** What is the purpose of our work together? (5 minutes)
   - Design math lessons.
   - Assess student math thinking.
   - Study mathematics content.

4. **Roles and Responsibilities:** What are our roles and responsibilities? (5 minutes)

   *Facilitator* (rotates each session)
   - Creates the learning agenda
   - Uses norms to keeps the conversation focused on agenda
   - Designates next session's facilitator

   *Recorder*
   - Documents learning and next steps
   - Designates next session's facilitator

   *Group Member*
   - Attends fully to conversation

   *Timekeeper*
   - Keeps track of time and informs facilitator

5. **Data:** What does data say? (15 minutes)
   - Use data sources (state assessments, benchmark) to identify what students know and demonstrate they can do.

*(continued)*

6. **Big Idea:** What is the mathematics "Big Idea" flow for the year? (15 minutes)

   - Use Common Core or state-specific standards, district scope and sequence, curriculum resources and make a quick sketch of how the math content progresses at the grade level.

   - Identify the Mathematical Practices of processes to develop in students.

7. **Reflection:** What did we learn today? (5 minutes)

   - Reflect on content and process.

     **Content:**

     Facilitator asks group to identify one to three points of learning to try in practice before the next team session (things to remember and try).

     Facilitator documents learning on one-pager.

     Facilitator documents next steps (things "to do" in practice and reflect on for next session).

     **Process:**

     What was the best part/most challenging part of the meeting?

8. **Looking Forward:** What are our next steps? (5 minutes)

   - What evidence will I bring to the next meeting?

   - When is the next meeting?

## Mathematics Content Learning Team

# Meeting 2 and Beyond Agenda
# (Key Questions)

The following questions can be used to design a Mathematics Content Learning Team agenda for the second meeting and beyond. Questions are used as a framework for creating agendas for meetings during the year.

1. **Introduction:** Who's in the room? How is everyone? (5 minutes)

2. **Actions:** What actions did you take from the last meeting? (5 minutes)
   Each person shares what action was taken and the result.

3. **Content-Specific:** Agendas after the first ten minutes depend on each team's purpose and focus. Teams will use some of the questions (not all depending on focus). (35 minutes)
   Here are some sample questions for team agendas:
   - What is the "Big Idea" flow in the upcoming unit?
   - What is the mathematics content identified in the Common Core or state-specific standards at our grade level?
   - What is the learning progression right before and after our grade level?
   - What is the math content we need to learn more about for teaching at our grade level?
   - What strategies do we use to solve a problem that students will be solving?
   - What strategies did students use?
   - What do students know and understand about the math content?
   - How are student demonstrating their understanding?

4. **Reflection:** What did we learn? (5 minutes)
   - Document one to three ideas to remember.

5. **Looking Ahead:** What actions do we take? (5 minutes)
   - What are our next steps?
   - When is the next meeting?

# Teacher-Focused Learning Agenda
# (Key Questions)

1. **Establish Norms:** What norms will help us learn together (first session)? (5 minutes)

2. **Revisit Norms:** Review norms (second and subsequent sessions). (2–3 minutes)
   - Which of our norms will you intentionally use today?
   - Which norm might be the most challenging to use today?

3. **Actions:** What are the actions taken and results noticed from the previous session (second and subsequent sessions)? (3 minutes)

4. **Standards:** What are the math standard(s) to study? (2 minutes)

5. **Content-Specific:** Study the mathematics of the standard. What is the knowledge of the mathematics that you need to guide student mastery of the standard? (25 minutes)

6. **Progressions:** Study the progression of the standard, looking at the grade level before and after. What changes from grade to grade? (5 minutes)

7. **Looking Forward:** What have we learned? What are our next steps?

# Student-Focused Learning Agenda
# (Key Questions)

1. **Establish Norms:** What norms will help us learn together (first session)? (5 minutes)

2. **Revisit Norms:** Review norms (second and subsequent sessions). (2–3 minutes)
   - Which of our norms will you intentionally use today?
   - Which norm might be the most challenging to use today?

3. **Actions:** What are the actions taken and results noticed from the previous session (second and subsequent sessions)? (3 minutes)

4. **Standards:** What are the math standard(s) students are to learn? (2 minutes)

5. **Assess:** Collaboratively assess student mastery of the standard. Put student work samples into three categories (e.g., "Got it," "Got some of it," "Got none of it"). (3 minutes)

6. **Identify Strengths:** What are the student strengths (knowledge, skills, understandings of the standard)? What do they know? (10 minutes)

7. **Identify Challenges:** What are the student misconceptions? (10 minutes)

8. **Identify Interventions:** How can we address student misconceptions?

9. **Identify Extensions:** What support and strategies can we use to expand student thinking?

10. **Looking Forward:** What have we learned? What are our next steps?

# Big Idea Flow

A "Big Idea" Flow describes the progression of important math concepts throughout a math unit, investigation, or lesson. The flow shows the development of math ideas of concepts and how they build. An effective way to build mathematics knowledge is to chart Big Idea Flows.

1. **Establish Norms:** Set norms for learning and behavior (first session). (5 minutes)

2. **Revisit Norms:** Review norms (Second and subsequent sessions). (2–3 minutes)
   - Which of our norms will you intentionally use today?
   - Which norm might be the most challenging to use today?

3. **Standards:** Identify the math standards students are to master in the upcoming unit of study

4. **Big Ideas:** Identify the "big math ideas" of the standards that are addressed in the unit, and how the concepts and skills develop during the unit

5. **Anticipate:** Anticipate student approaches to the standards. Where will they be successful? Where will they struggle?

6. **Time:** Identify approximate times to spend on each "big idea." Allow more time on concepts that students might be more cognitively demanding.

7. **Identify Interventions:** Articulate supports and strategies to address student struggles.

8. **Identify Extensions:** Articulate supports and strategies to expand student thinking.

9. **Looking Ahead:** Identify and document learning and action steps.

# Tips for a Successful Mathematics Content Learning Team Meeting

1. **Do make small talk.** Human connections during the first few minutes of a meeting are not wasted time; they put us in touch with each other.

2. **Start and end on time.** Try passing out a small reward (like a pen or pad of sticky notes) to everyone who is present at the appointed time.

3. **Post agreed-to learning and behavior norms in the meeting space for easy reference.**

4. **Be prepared.** Have each participant bring at least one student sample or math problem related to the learning focus to share and discuss at the meeting.

5. **Have the standards handy.** If possible, keep a copy in the meeting room, or agree that the facilitator or recorder always brings a copy.

6. **Keep it positive.** Frame problems as challenges, seek multiple solutions, and always bring the conversation back to the primary purpose: improving student learning. Avoid using *you*; use *we* or *I*. Remember that relationships are built over time, but can be destroyed with one word or in less than one minute.

7. **Listen fully and ask questions.** Rather than assume you know what a person is trying to say, ask questions to clarify his or her ideas.

8. **Rotate roles so leadership is distributed and the meeting is not dependent on one person.**

9. **Use a Parking Lot for issues that need more time for conversation.** These issues can be addressed at the beginning of the next meeting.

10. **Keep the focus on ideas, not people.**

11. **Celebrate!** Do something enjoyable to mark occasions of success, learning, and perseverance!

# Chapter 3

# Shared Classroom Experience

It is common practice for teachers of the same grade to plan together on many campuses, but how can they be sure that planning together translates into successful teaching practices? One benefit of using Shared Classroom Experiences, when teachers not only plan together but also teach and learn together in collaboration with a coach and/or administrator, is consistency in practice. There are many more benefits! In fact, done well, a Shared Classroom Experience can be a vital and transformative professional learning experience for everyone involved.

In this chapter, we discuss how students, teachers, coaches, and principals can learn from participating in a Shared Classroom Experience. We

- Offer a variety of video clips of actual Shared Classroom Experiences
- Provide step-by-step guidelines for planning and implementing Shared Classroom Experiences
- Share tools, agendas, and reproducibles
- Suggest strategies for ensuring successful experiences

We end the chapter with a "Your Turn" that gives you an opportunity to design a productive Shared Classroom Experience at your school.

## Overview

## Tools You Can Use

Videos can be streamed by registering this product at mathsolutions.com/myvideos. See page xxiii for instructions.

Tools You Can Use (Reproducibles) appear at the end of the chapter and are also available online at mathsolutions.com/givemefivereproducibles.

# How It Looks in Practice

Many teachers at Travis Elementary work together as grade-level collaborative teams. They plan together and discuss which lessons they will teach and when they will teach them. They also share ideas across grade levels at regular Mathematics Vertical Learning Team meetings (see Chapter 4). Although this collaboration is helpful, teachers realize that teaching together and inviting the math coach and principal to be involved by observing student learning is also powerful, so they decided to implement Shared Classroom Experiences at their school. They first held Meeting 1: Planning the Lesson. The following video clips illustrate the next three meetings they held as part of the Shared Learning Cycle (Meeting 2: Briefing Observers, Meeting 3: Teaching the Lesson, and Meeting 4: Reflecting on the Lesson).

**▶ Video Clip 3.1**

To view this video clip, scan the QR code or access via mathsolutions.com/GMF31

## A Shared Classroom Experience: Briefing Observers

This clip shows Meeting 2 of the Shared Classroom Experience cycle, in which a first-grade teacher and a second-grade teacher meet with the principal and math coach, who will observe student thinking and learning during the lesson. Consider the following questions:

- Who leads the meeting?
- How do the principal, coach, and teachers interact with each other?
- What is the benefit of having this type of meeting?

See the authors' reflections on these questions in the Appendix.

**Video Clip 3.2**

## A Shared Classroom Experience: Teaching the Lesson

This clip shows the two teachers in Video Clip 3.1 teaching the lesson together while the principal and math coach observe. Consider the following questions:

- What do you notice about the roles of the classroom teachers?
- What do the principal and math coach do as students work in partners?
- What connections do you notice between Meeting 2 (Video Clip 3.1) and the lesson (considered Meeting 3 of the Shared Classroom Experience cycle)?

 To view this video clip, scan the QR code or access via mathsolutions.com/GMF32

See the authors' reflections on these questions in the Appendix.

 **Video Clip 3.3**

## A Shared Classroom Experience: Reflecting on the Lesson

This clip shows the teachers, principal, and math coach from Video Clips 3.1 and 3.2 now debriefing about students' learning as part of Meeting 4 in the Shared Classroom Experience cycle. Consider the following questions:

- Compare the teachers' expectations for the lesson with what happened during the lesson. What did they learn about their students?
- What kinds of ideas were generated at the meeting? How will they affect students' learning?
- How do you think the collaboration benefited the teachers? The math coach? The principal? The students?

 To view this video clip, scan the QR code or access via mathsolutions.com/GMF33

See the authors' reflections on these questions in the Appendix.

*(continued)*

**Your Turn** **Defining a Shared Classroom Experience**

Think about words that come to mind when you hear the term *Shared Classroom Experience*. Words probably depend on your experiences with peer teaching, coaching, or other types of observations. Consider how a Shared Classroom Experience could prove useful and productive. List some of the words that come to mind here:

_____

_____

_____

Based on your ideas gleaned from the videos, write a definition in your own words of a Shared Classroom Experience.

_____

_____

_____

# What Is a Shared Classroom Experience?

**The Equation**

Shared (have something in common with someone else)
+
Classroom (heterogeneous group of students)
+
Experience (knowledge gained through being involved in something)
=
Mathematics Success

## The Definition

A Shared Classroom Experience involves two or more educators collaborating to plan and teach a lesson together, and inviting other teachers, coaches, and/or the principal to share the experience of the lesson. A Shared Classroom

Experience is not designed to "fix" bad teachers; its purpose is to empower effective teachers to become more reflective and effective. In this way, a Shared Classroom Experience is an authentic, professional learning experience. The experience culminates with all participants gathering to reflect on student learning. It consists of a cycle of four meetings:

### The Cycle of a Shared Classroom Experience

1. **Planning the Lesson** (30–45 minutes): Two teachers and/or a math coach plan a lesson they will team-teach, choosing a topic and exploring ways to teach and differentiate the learning together.

2. **Briefing Observers** (10 minutes): The two team-teachers brief observers about what to expect from the lesson. The teachers explain their learning targets, describe the lesson flow, state what they expect students to understand, and direct observers to pay particular attention to what they expect will be points of difficulty for students. They may also share with the observers some questions or prompts they could use as they listen to conversations between students.

   For more on the role of observers, see page 136.

3. **Teaching the Lesson** (30–60 minutes): The two team-teachers facilitate the lesson while the principal and math coach, and maybe other teachers, observe and interact with students as they work. The principal and coach listen to what students say during the lesson to help inform teachers about students' learning and challenges.

4. **Reflecting on the Lesson** (15–20 minutes): The team-teachers and observers gather to reflect on the lesson, identifying what they learned about student thinking and learning, and suggest possible interventions and supports to advance student learning.

The two team-teachers can be a classroom teacher and a math coach, or two classroom teachers from the same or different grades. Observers can include the principal, math coach, and/or other teachers at the same or different grade levels. The goal is a professional learning experience in which all participants learn more about math content and how it builds over the years, explore different instructional strategies, and gain insight into students' thinking processes and any challenges or difficulties they have with the content.

## The Role of Observers in the Shared Classroom Experience: Kidwatcher

Inviting the math coach, principal, or other teachers to participate in a Shared Classroom Experience is the key factor that separates Shared Classroom Experiences from peer teaching. Both are formal designs for professional learning that build teachers' knowledge and skills, and promote different ways of thinking about mathematics planning and teaching (Easton 2015, Learning Forward 2011). Both learning designs involve teachers sharing practice together through planning, teaching, assessing, and reflecting; both promote experiential learning and collaborative inquiry toward shared goals for students' math learning. But, involving additional educators to observe the lesson makes an enormous difference in the learning experience. Although we call them *observers*, it is not in the traditional sense of observing the teacher with the intent to critique or evaluate. Rather, their participation in the Shared Classroom Experience is more that of *kidwatcher*, a term we borrow from Yetta Goodman that is typically used in literacy classrooms (Owocki and Goodman 2002). Owocki and Goodman (2002) note that the primary goals of kidwatching are to gain insight into children's learning by (1) observing and documenting what students know and can do; (2) documenting their ways of constructing and conveying knowledge; and (3) planning curriculum and instruction that support individual strengths and needs. One teacher in a classroom may kidwatch her students during practice, but imagine how much more powerful it is to have three or four or even five educators closely observing students at work, documenting the thinking and strategy use they see, and brainstorming together ideas for future instruction based on what they see. That is the power of the Shared Classroom Experience.

## Research Says . . .

The Shared Classroom Experience has its roots in research on professional learning communities (PLCs). According to Hall and Hord (2011), schools with a culture that is not open to change do not have success in improving student learning. Research has indicated the importance of considering five dimensions of a professional learning community as guidelines to creating an environment conducive to change for improvement (Hall and Hord 2011, Little 2003, Supovitz 2002, Hord 1997). The dimensions are interactive and include shared values and vision, intentional collective learning and application, supportive and shared leadership, supportive conditions, and shared personal practice. The Shared Classroom Experience, as well as Mathematics Content and Vertical Learning Team structures, are specialized forms of PLCs.

As a researcher and committed supporter and site-based consultant for school change and improvement, Shirley Hord is a consistent advocate of school improvement and believes the PLC is our most powerful strategy for increasing teaching effectiveness and, consequently, kids' learning. She has been nicknamed "the Vigilante of PLC" because of "my untiring efforts to help people to understand that the PLC is about learning in a group setting for adults" (pers. comm. with Shirley Hord, August 2010). Hord claims the PLC offers a powerful response to expectations for increased knowledge and improved instructional practice. The power of the PLC is located in its focus on improving an entire school staff, as opposed to improving a few teachers, so that all students—not just some students—experience high-quality teaching and learning and ultimately achieve at high levels (Hord and Hirsh 2008).

For a Vygotskyian perspective, consider that, as learners participate in a broad range of joint activities and internalize the effects of working together, they acquire new strategies and knowledge of the world and culture. Vygotsky was concerned with the unity and interdependence of learning and development (Tudge and Schrimsher 2003, Vygotsky 1986).

# Scheduling Shared Classroom Experiences

*"The Shared Classroom Experience helps everyone to be equal partners. It is not a hierarchal relationship. Everybody comes in with the shared goal of listening to student thinking, collecting student strategies, and figuring out how can we work together to move towards student success."*

—Courtney Blackmon, math coach

Shared Classroom Experiences can be a relevant, useful, and meaningful means of supporting changes in teaching for student-focused mathematics learning if they become a integral part of a school's culture. For that to happen, Shared Classroom Experiences must become a regular component of a school's professional learning program. Although they may be mandated by a district's Action Plan, Shared Classroom Experiences will not take root and effect change without significant teacher buy-in and administrative support at the building level.

To begin this process, we recommend that a math coach or teacher leader work alongside an interested and motivated teacher or teachers in a Shared Classroom Experience, inviting the principal to participate. As educators collaborate in planning, pool their observations of student learning, and strategize about next steps together, it creates a positive energy that spreads; as teachers see the impact on student learning, they become interested in participating themselves.

Ideally, each teacher would participate in one Shared Classroom Experience per semester, but it takes time to build up to that level of participation. We have also found that after teaching together in one classroom, teachers are often eager to work together in other classrooms. Limiting them to one Shared Classroom Experience only in this case makes teachers feel less supported when they need help, and it takes away some of the trust that has been established, so it's important to allow and even encourage multiple Shared Classroom Experiences when teachers seek to initiate them.

As Shared Classroom Experiences become commonplace on a campus, they can be placed on the calendar before school starts during or after the Strategic Planning Session (see Chapter 1). Concepts that are hard to teach or hard to learn should be the target of these experiences, but let teachers add to these dates if they stumble with something during the school year. Teachers should see the experiences as ways to get help or learn more about their students.

## It Really Can Happen . . . Insights from the Field

The Shared Classroom Experience helps to create experiential learning for principals, math coaches, and teachers together as they collaborate for a shared goal: improving student math learning. But, we've found it also fosters empathy among grade levels. All too often, principals, coaches, and teachers participate separately in their respective roles, and their interactions might involve evaluation and judgment. We've heard teachers blame the previous grade level for not having prepared students, yet after spending time with the lower grade-level teacher—planning, watching students at work, and understanding what the students have learned—they often become more tolerant and understanding. Sometimes, for struggling students, it is simply a matter of inconsistency in vocabulary that causes problems, and if teachers know how the concept was presented previously, they can go back and make the link to help students remember what they know.

When we began Shared Classroom Experiences, we assumed teachers should go only into a classroom that was one grade level up or down, but teachers demonstrated they could learn no matter what the relation between grade levels. The conversation between teachers before and after the classroom was the critical learning point. We noticed an additional benefit of crossing multiple grade levels. As teachers became acquainted or reacquainted with students, they began to show a continued interest in how the students were progressing in their math knowledge after the experience. Knowing the same students, not just by name, but by strengths and struggles, allows teachers more opportunities for conversations about student learning, which in turn reinforces the vision and goals, and strengthens the school.

### ▶ Video Clip 3.4

 To view this video clip, scan the QR code or access via mathsolutions.com/ GMF34

### A Shared Classroom Experience in Action

At Travis Elementary, both fourth- and fifth-grade students were having trouble comparing fractions, so fifth-grade teacher Mrs. Easley and fourth-grade teacher Mrs. Davis decided to have a Shared Classroom Experience to gain insight into students' difficulties and to generate ideas to support their learning. They asked the math coach and principal to participate in the Shared Classroom Experience and to contribute their insights and knowledge. As you watch this clip, consider the following questions:

- What do you notice about the relationships among the teachers, math coach, and principal?
- How does the collaboration affect the teaching and learning?
- How might you expect this experience to impact future teaching and learning about fractions in the fourth and fifth grades?

See the authors' reflections on these questions in the Appendix.

**Your Turn**

In thinking about how Shared Classroom Experiences would support your school, consider the following question:

What actions are currently being taken at your campus to ensure all teachers teach to influence student learning?

_____

_____

_____

# What Is the Agenda for the Shared Classroom Experience?

Rather than listening to a presentation and jotting down strategies that never make it back to the classroom, this collaborative structure allows teachers to learn about their students' mathematical understanding and it gives them time to solve problems regarding ways to differentiate with another teacher, math coach, or principal. In addition, the Shared Classroom Experience is the vehicle that translates the goals of the Vision Statement and Action Plan (created in Strategic Planning Sessions; see Chapter 1) into actual classroom situations with real students. It takes goals from the abstract to the concrete for everyone; even those not involved initially in the Shared Classroom Experience will hear about learning that is happening in classrooms on campus.

See Reproducible 16: Ten-Step Guide to an Effective Shared Classroom Experience.

| Meeting 1: Planning the Lesson | Meeting 2: Briefing Observers | Meeting 3: Teaching the Lessons | Meeting 4: Reflecting on the Lesson |
|---|---|---|---|
| Step 1: What are the learning objectives and student needs? | Step 1: What's today's lesson? | Step 1: Who is joining us today? | Step 1: What were students doing during the lesson? |
| Step 2: What lesson will best support student learning? | Step 2: What should observers focus on? | Step 2: What is the lesson? | Step 2: What challenges did students have? |
| Step 3: What is the role of the observers? | Step 3: How should observers participate? | Step 3: What are students learning? | Step 3: How can these student challenges be overcome? |

## Why Are Shared Classroom Experiences Important?

**Shared Classroom Experiences . . .**

1. Support moving the shared vision, goals, agreements, commitments, and language expressed in the Vision Statement and Action Plan to the concrete world of the classroom

2. Promote a collaborative culture for learning and growing professionally

3 Build trust among teachers and administrators who have shared the classroom experience

4. Create a common experience on which participants can reflect

5. Allow teachers to see the development of the trajectory across the standards through the grade levels

Each part of the Shared Classroom Experience meeting cycle is driven by the goal of improving student achievement by better understanding students' thinking processes, understandings, misconceptions, and challenges. The focus is on students, which keeps the focus off teaching, which helps teachers feel less defensive and more willing to make adjustments that might impact student learning. The agenda for each of the four meetings (Planning the Lesson, Briefing Observers, Teaching the Lesson, and Reflecting on the Lesson) that comprise a Shared Classroom Experience is described in the following section.

### Video Clip 3.5

To view this video clip, scan the QR code or access via mathsolutions.com/GMF35

### The Power of a Shared Classroom Experience

As you watch this clip, which features a kindergarten Shared Classroom Experience that also became the focus of a Mathematics Vertical Learning Team Meeting (see Chapter 4), consider the following questions:

- What evidence do you see of a collaborative culture?
- What do you notice about the interaction of the adults with the students during the lesson? About student engagement with the lesson?
- How would participating in a Shared Classroom Experience benefit you?

See the authors' reflections on these questions in the Appendix.

## Meeting 1  Planning the Lesson

**Approximate Time**   30–45 minutes

**Scheduling**   This meeting should occur the day before or the day the lesson will be taught.

### Objectives

- Identify learning objectives and student needs.
- Select the lesson and materials to address objectives and needs.
- Document the plan for observers.

| Step | Documents to Create |
|---|---|
| Step 1:  What are the learning objectives and student needs? | Lesson Plan |
| Step 2:  What lesson will best support student learning? | Lesson Plan (continue building from Step 1) |
| Step 3:  What is the role of the observers? | Observer Protocol |

## Step 1:  What Are the Learning Objectives and Student Needs? (10 minutes)

*Objective:  Identify learning objectives and student needs*

The first step is to choose the learning objectives to be addressed during the lesson and consider students' needs in relation to the objectives. For example, the second-grade team at Travis Elementary wanted students to practice adding and subtracting numbers fluently within one hundred using strategies based on place value and the relationship between addition and subtraction. The objective should be recorded on a Lesson Plan; Reproducible 17, Lesson Planning Tool, can be used to guide the planning.

**Key Question**

- What difficulties do students typically encounter with these learning objectives?

See Reproducible 17, Lessons Planning Tool on page 159.

**Key Questions**

- Which instructional strategies can we use to teach the objective?
- In which practice can we engage students?
- How can we check students' understanding?

## Step 2: What Lesson Will Best Support Student Learning? (30 minutes)

*Objective: Select the lesson and materials to address objectives and needs*

Next, educators collaborate to design a lesson to teach the objectives, taking into account the specific needs of their students. They may draw on

- Curricular resources, including lesson plans and manipulatives
- Supplemental resources, such as games and interactive websites
- Strategies from professional reading or other learning experiences

This is an opportunity for educators to share and discuss instructional strategies and materials in a nonthreatening way; the focus is on designing the best lesson to support the specific students in a classroom. For example, when Ms. Corey, the math coach at Lamar Elementary, met with the first- and second-grade teachers to plan the lesson on using place-value understanding to add and subtract numbers within one hundred, she brought the *Number Balances* problem that she had found in a book, and shared it with the teachers. The teachers thought it would be a fun and engaging way for students to solidify and practice their understanding of using place value to add and subtract numbers, so they decided to use it in their lesson. (You can see a video of the lesson in which the *Number Balances Puzzle* as used in Video Clip 3.2.)

Teachers need to decide who will facilitate each part of the lesson so nothing gets left out and they aren't "stepping on each other." All lessons have definite parts, and each teacher should have near-equal participation. This is also the fun part of teaching together. Teachers can role-play, with one struggling to understand and asking students or the other teacher to give clarification or suggest strategies, and the other teacher can verbalize the metacognition to help students understand strategies, thinking aloud to solve a problem. The teachers can play a game together to model for students. There are all kinds of creative ways to engage students with team-teaching. See Figure 3–1 for a sample completed lesson using Reproducible 17, Lesson Planning Tool.

# Lesson Planning Tool

1. What is my learning target?

   The student will be able to show how to balance the numbers on the scale. Student language: I can show how to balance numbers on the scale.

2. What practice problem(s) will go with this objective? What strategy will I utilize for solving the problem(s)?

   We will model the number puzzle to the whole class. The students will have a chance to share their thinking and strategies, as well as work with a partner and independently. Sentence frames will be used to allow students to speak and listen using correct mathematics vocabulary.

3. What tools, technology, or other resources will I integrate to increase student engagement?

   100s chart, base 10 blocks, number lines, sentence frames

For your own Lesson Planning Tool template, see Reproducible 17.

**FIGURE 3–1. Sample Completed Lesson Planning Tool**

## Step 3: What Is the Role of the Observers? (10 minutes)

*Objective: Document the plan for observers*

When the Lesson Plan is designed, using the Lesson Planning Tool (Reproducible 17) or another template, consider how to share the plan with the observers you will invite and what role you would like them to take during the lesson. Reproducible 18, Observer Protocol can be used for this purpose; it summarizes the learning objective and lesson flow, identifies areas you anticipate students will grasp and those with which they will struggle, describes strategies students may use, and suggests ways for observers to engage with students during the practice portion of the lesson. (See Figure 3–2 on page 146 for a sample completed Observer Protocol.)

**Key Questions**

- What do we want observers to pay attention to during the lesson?
- How do we want the observers to participate in the lesson?

## Meeting 2   Briefing Observers

*"I love watching the students learn from each other. That is one of my favorite parts—just seeing how much students can learn from each other."*

—Jill Faubion, principal

Watch excerpts from Meeting 2, Briefing Observers, in Video Clip 3.1.

**Approximate Time**    10 minutes

**Scheduling**    This meeting should occur shortly before the lesson is to be taught.

### Objectives

- Share the lesson with observers.
- Inform observers on what they should focus on.
- Inform observers on how to participate in the lesson.

| Step | Documents to Share |
|------|--------------------|
| Step 1: What's today's lesson?<br>Step 2: What should observers focus on? | Observer Protocol (completed in Meeting 1) |
| Step 3: How should observers participate? | Observer Protocol (completed in Meeting 1) |
| | Reflective Protocol: complete |

## Step 1:  What's Today's Lesson? (5 minutes)

*Objective:  Share the lesson with observers*

Give each observer a copy of the Observer Protocol completed in Meeting 1. Review the learning objective and lesson flow, then discuss what parts of the lesson you think will be easy for students and what parts might prove challenging. Invite observers to ask any questions they may have about the lesson.

**Key Questions**

• What is the learning objective?

• What is the lesson flow?

• What challenges might students have with the lesson?

## Step 2:  What Should Observers Focus On? (2–3 minutes)

*Objective:  Inform observers on what they should focus on*

Now share with the observers specifically what you as the team-teachers would like them to focus as they kidwatch (see page 136). This might be related to the challenges you anticipate students will have with the content, or perhaps it's related to an instructional goal you're working to reach, such as including more partner talk or integrating the use of manipulatives. In our second-grade example, teachers wanted observers to listen for the specific strategies students used to decompose one hundred into two numbers and how students recombined the two numbers to total one hundred.

**Key Question**

• What should observers pay attention to during the lesson?

## Step 3:  How Should Observers Participate? (2–3 minutes)

*Objective:  Inform observers on how to participate in the lesson*

The last part of this meeting is to suggest to the observers how they might interact with students. Share Reflective Protocol with observers to think about and then complete during the lesson (see Reproducible 19). The observers just watch during the direct instruction portion and then can begin to circulate around the room, listening in and interacting with students to discover their thinking during the practice portion. If there are not specific prompts for them, observers can always ask students "What are you thinking about X?" or "Is there another way to do that?" or "Why does that make sense?" to get at student thinking. Listening and recording notes about conversations (using the Reflective Protocol) among students is a valuable service to teachers because it provides a window into the student's thinking.

**Key Question**

• How should observers interact with students?

See Reproducible 19: Reflective Protocol.

For a blank template of this Observer Protocol, see Reproducible 18.

# Observer Protocol

## Observer Protocol (Teacher led)

1. Today, the learning targets for the lesson are:  to show how to balance numbers on a scale.

2. The lesson flow includes:  introducing number puzzles and modeling problems to the whole group, sharing strategies, working with a partner and then independently

3. I'm (We're) anticipating students will understand:  the concept of balancing the number puzzle   and might be challenged on precisely balancing the numbers and part–part–whole number relationships.

4. I'm (We're) anticipating student strategies for solving the problem might include:  counting by 1s or 10s, using 100s chart, base 10 blocks, number line.

5. Strategies to engage students include:  use of the term puzzle, modeling and recording, use of manipulatives, and sentence frames

6. Comments and/or questions:

   Where can the depth of rigor be increased? What additional supports are needed for emergent bilingual students? What work samples will be collected for us to look at after the lesson?

**FIGURE 3–2.  Sample Completed Shared Classroom Experience: Observer Protocol**

## Meeting 3  Teaching the Lesson

**Approximate Time**   45–60 minutes

**Scheduling**   Lesson is taught during regular math class time.

**Objectives**

- Introduce coteacher and observers.
- Teach the lesson.
- Observe student learning.

Watch excerpts of a lesson during a Shared Classroom Experience in Video 3.2.

| Step | Documents to Revisit or Complete |
|---|---|
| Step 1: Who is joining us today? | Lesson Plan: revisit as needed |
| Step 2: What is the lesson? | Observer Protocol: revisit as needed |
| Step 3: What are students learning? | Reflective Protocol: complete |

## Step 1:  Who Is Joining Us Today? (1–2 minutes)

*Objective:  Introduce coteacher and observers*

Take a minute or two to introduce your coteacher and any observers and to explain why they're in the classroom. Ideally, the classroom teacher will have prepared students for the experience in advance; if not, brief introductions will do.

**Key Question**

- How can we make students feel comfortable with the coteacher and observers?

## Step 2:  What Is the Lesson? (40–55 minutes)

*Objective:  Teach the lesson*

Observers simply watch the direct instruction, paying attention to student learning and making notes in the Reflective Protocol as appropriate. When students work independently or collaboratively, observers can circulate and ask them questions to elicit their thinking, following any guidelines set out in the Observer Protocol completed from Meeting 2.

**Key Questions**

- What is easy for students?
- What is challenging for students?
- How does the flow of the lesson work?

**Key Questions**

- How is the learning going?
- What areas are secure?
- What areas need further practice and/or reteaching?

## Step 3: What Are Students Learning? (3–5 minutes)

*Objective: Observe student learning*

Of course, kidwatching (see page 136) and assessing student learning happens throughout a lesson, but it is important to take time toward the end of a lesson to summarize and document how the learning went. This may be through a formative assessment that is part of the Lesson Plan, more informally through anecdotal notes, or by using Reproducible 19, Reflective Protocol.

## Meeting 4 — Reflecting on the Lesson

Watch excerpts from a Reflective Meeting in Video Clip 3.3.

*"It's very nice to have another teacher in the room teaching my students; this allows me to stay on the side and think more about my students' understanding. What do they seem to misunderstand? Where do we go next from here? Sometimes when you're the only one teaching, you might miss those little moments."*

—Tatiana Greer, second-grade teacher

**Approximate Time**  15–20 minutes

**Scheduling**  Ideally, this meeting should occur the same day as the lesson, but no more than two days after it.

### Objectives

- Summarize student learning.
- Identify challenges students had with the content.
- Explore ideas for helping students overcome challenges.

| Step | Documents to Revisit |
|---|---|
| Step 1: What were students doing during the lesson? | Reflective Protocol (partially completed in Meeting 3) |
| Step 2: What challenges did students have? | |
| Step 3: How can these student challenges be overcome? | |

# Step 1: **What Were Students Doing during the Lesson?** (10–15 minutes)

*Objective: **Summarize student learning***

**Key Question**

• What did students learn from the lesson?

Make sure everyone brings their Reflective Protocol (see Reproducible 19) to the meeting. The reflection conversation begins with the teachers who taught the lesson. What did they observe students doing during the lesson? What evidence do they have about students' understanding of the standards? What do they want to celebrate? Did anything surprise them? The conversation continues with each member sharing an anecdote or student work sample. For example, the second-grade team at Lamar Elementary put students into groups based on student work samples: "got it," "didn't get it," "got some of it." On this day, ten students "got it"; they balanced the puzzle correctly using either place-value understanding to add or subtract or by using the subtraction algorithm, and they could show their strategy so others could understand. Five students could balance the puzzle, but could not show their strategy. Three students could not balance the puzzle and showed no understanding of addition and subtraction with place value.

See Reproducible 19 for a blank template to use as a Reflective Protocol.

**Key Questions**

- What challenges did students have with the learning?
- Did the supports in place help address those challenges?

## Step 2: What Challenges Did Students Have? (15–20 minutes)

*Objective: Identify challenges students had with the content*

Use evidence of student learning to identify specific challenges students had with the content. For instance, in our second-grade example, challenges for students included not being able to use place-value strategies, not using the algorithm correctly, not knowing whether to add or subtract, and not understanding that the missing number was part of the larger number. One teacher reflected on a student who would add the larger number and the addend together to find the missing addend. One student counted on by tens and got stuck when he needed to start counting by ones to equal the larger number.

**Key Question**

- How can we help students overcome the challenges the content presented?

## Step 3: How Can These Student Challenges Be Overcome? (15–20 minutes)

*Objective: Explore ideas for helping students overcome challenges*

Now the team shares ideas for helping students overcome their challenges. In our second-grade example, the teachers discussed the supports needed for students to develop a greater understanding of place value, how to use place value to add and subtract, and how students can solidify their understanding of the relationship between addition and subtraction. They turned to two resources—*Elementary and Middle School Mathematics: Teaching Developmentally* (Van de Walle et al. 2012) and *About Teaching Mathematics: A K–8 Resource* (Burns 2015)—where they located activities that would support students' conceptual understanding of these skills.

## It Can Really Happen . . . Insights from the Field

Reflective conversations often result in classroom teachers thinking about different ways to design the lesson next time based on how students performed. Other educators are a wonderful resource and can share ideas that have worked well for them and offer feedback on parts of a lesson that didn't work as well. Having a set of instructional strategies that have been tried, improved on, and tried again, is a powerful tool in any teacher's toolbox, and participating in Shared Classroom Experiences and sharing during Reflective Discussions is a way to make this happen.

For example, in Travis Elementary, a fifth-grade teacher participated with a third-grade teacher in a Shared Classroom Experience about elapsed time. During Meeting 4: Reflecting on the Lesson, the fifth-grade teacher realized she had access to some manipulatives the third-grade teacher did not have, or even know about. The fifth-grade teacher offered to share them with the third-grade classes, and even meet with the all the third-grade teachers to explain how they were used. The fifth-grade teacher later told the math coach, "If they do not understand this in third grade, I am going to have to go back and reteach it before I can move on in fifth grade." This was a win/win situation for third- and fifth-grade teachers.

In addition, Shared Classroom Experiences allow teachers to see the math coach and principal as partners in the classroom, which contributes to the collaborative approach mandated by the Vision Statement and Action Plan (see Chapter 1). It is easier to ask for help with a struggling student when there is trust among the educators on a campus. Sometimes teachers forget that administrators began their career as teachers, and the administrators with whom we worked were glad to be back in the teaching role for a short time. Holding meetings before and after teaching the Shared Classroom Experience lesson gives the principal and coach the opportunity to share some of the instructional tools they have seen across the campus or have used themselves as teachers. Having seen the principal and coach as a teacher levels the playing field for teachers and helps them feel more comfortable in sharing when they are stressed because a student is having trouble. It also gives the principal insights into student learning that can inform conversations about struggling students with parents, Response-to-Intervention teams, or other teachers.

To illustrate, consider this example of an elementary principal with a secondary background who was struggling to understand why the kindergarten teacher's students were not progressing as quickly as she thought they should. This principal had only been in kindergarten classrooms as the principal, never as a teacher. After participating in a Shared Classroom Experience and having first-hand experience at working with a group of kindergarten students having trouble with one-to-one correspondence, the principal began to understand the frustration the teacher was feeling. This principal was so interested in the issue that she began to read professional books and learned about the counting strategies necessary to learn in kindergarten. She realized the kindergarten needed more manipulatives and math games, and she found some money for kindergarten teachers to use for their math needs. The kindergarten teachers felt supported and, with a principal so eager to help, the teachers were very excited to open up to the principal about successes and struggles. This spread throughout the school and the climate of the school changed for the better.

## The Framework for a Shared Classroom Experience

**Before the lesson, the math coach or classroom teacher . . .**

1. *Invites coteachers and observers to participate in a Shared Classroom Experience and sets dates and times for four meetings.*

   Planning the Lesson: Occurs one to two days before the lesson is taught.

   Briefing the Observers Meeting: Occurs before the lesson is taught.

   Teaching the Lesson

   Reflective Discussion: Occurs the same day as the lesson is taught, or no more than two days after.

2. *Works with a coteacher to choose and design the lesson.* Coteachers plan the lesson, gather materials, and decide who will teach each component of the lesson. They complete the Lesson Plan and Observer Protocol to share with observers.

3. *Briefs observers on the lesson.* Coteachers share the lesson with observers, identifying what they would like observers to focus on during their kidwatching (see page 136).

**During the lesson, coteachers . . .**

4. *Introduce visitors to the students.* The classroom teacher introduces the coteacher and any observers to set students at ease during the experience.

5. *Teach the lesson.*

**During the lesson, observers and coteachers . . .**

6. *Listen to student responses, looking for evidence of understanding or misconceptions.* Observers can document what they see using a Reflective Protocol.

7. *Gather student artifacts to take to the Reflective Discussion if appropriate.* Anecdotal notes and examples of student work are useful artifacts that can spark helpful conversations about student learning.

**After the lesson, observers and coteachers . . .**

8. *Gather for Meeting 4: Reflecting on the Lesson.* Ideally, this conversation is held in the classroom where the lesson was taught, on the same day or as soon after as possible, but within two days of the lesson.

9. *Have a conversation about what was seen and learned during the lesson based on artifacts gathered during the lesson.* Evidence of learning should be the focus of this conversation.

10. *Complete a Reflective Protocol.* During the conversation, participants can discuss possible next steps and supports, documenting them along with instructional strategies and other ideas the group considers to strengthen their professional learning.

# Strategies for Success

Shared Classroom Experiences help build relationships among teachers, coaches, and administrators as they provide insight into students' mathematic thinking. Because they are situated in the classroom and engage participants directly with students, these experiences are truly foundational to any professional learning initiative. Here are a few strategies we recommend for making these experiences the most successful they can be.

## Empower Teachers to Lead Shared Classroom Experiences

If your campus does not have a math coach or teacher leader to initiate and guide Shared Classroom Experiences, ask teachers who are willing to take risks to learn and grow to try it out. Every campus has teachers who are natural risk takers and won't mind being the first to try this new structure. We began with teachers who were already working closely with the coach or each other. They were risk takers and eager to learn from each other.

## Use Formative Assessments

Incorporate formative assessments into Shared Classroom Experiences to have documentation of student learning. Here are three formative assessment strategies that help identify students' level of understanding during and after the lessons:

1. **Exit Ticket.** Give students a sticky note at the end of the lesson and ask them to answer a specific math question related to the lesson.
2. **Student Work Samples.** Collect student work that was done during the lesson.
3. **Anecdotal Notes.** Take anecdotal notes about students' responses to focused questions that elicit student thinking about key math concepts and skills.

## Support Teachers as They Open Their Classrooms to Observation

Think about another adult sitting in your classroom. For many years that person was an administrator who came to evaluate you or a coach who came to tell you whether you did a good job of teaching or how you could improve. No one ever came by to spend time helping you with your students. It is scary to open your classroom to visitors who will watch you teach; it makes you very vulnerable. So you should anticipate that the first time or two, teachers will be nervous about participating in a Shared Classroom Experience.

If you are the administrator, remind teachers that you began as a teacher. You might recall and share a time when you were vulnerable, made a mistake, or were being observed as a teacher. Assure the teacher this opportunity gives you a chance to experience what it feels like to be a teacher again; let the students see you as a teacher, not just an authority figure. It is very important for you to act as a teacher and not an administrator during the time in the classroom. Never use something you observed during this time as an evaluation of the teacher. This is not a time to observe teaching; it is a time to observe student learning. If you make the mistake and criticize the teacher, word will spread and you will not have any teacher who wants you to come into the classroom. It cannot be emphasized enough that student learning and supporting the teacher are your goals for these sessions as an administrator.

## Keep the Reflective Discussion Focused on Evidence of Student Learning

Use the notes taken as you listened and observed students to guide this conversation. Keep the conversation focused on what the students understand and what they struggle to understand, including evidence of those understandings and confusions. This conversation should not be dominated by any one person

**Video Clip 3.3**

To view this video clip, scan the QR code or access via mathsolutions.com/ GMF33

### A Shared Classroom Experience: Reflecting on the Lesson, Revisited

Rewatch Video Clip 3.3 and consider the following questions:

- What kinds of evidence did participants discuss?
- How did referring to evidence affect the discussion?

See the authors' reflections on these questions in the Appendix.

and, as teachers begin to see this is a nonjudgmental conversation truly designed to help them with their students, they will relax and begin to open their classroom even more. Be sure to share any prompting you did to help students understand and whether it was successful.

## Encourage Shared Classroom Experiences across Grade Levels

When the Shared Classroom Experience is between different grade levels, it affords participating teachers the opportunity to see the development of a concept across the standards. They see the importance of being certain the concept is developed to the depth and complexity required in their grade level. If teachers don't understand how a concept students are required to learn is built on in future learning, the result can be students who have a shaky foundation. After a Shared Classroom Experience, teachers who have had time in a grade level below their own will be able to use that experience in their classroom to help students who are not ready for grade-level requirements. They can remember the lessons used at the lower levels; likewise, a teacher who has high achievers may use lessons they saw in an upper grade. This again adds to strategies available to teachers even when they have to raise or lower the level according to student needs.

## Include First-Year Teachers in Shared Classroom Experiences

After Shared Classroom Experiences become a normal part of professional learning on a campus, they are valuable for first-year teachers. These teachers have the opportunity to practice lesson design, learn how a collaborative relationship between professional educators works, and benefit from reflective discussions with more experienced teachers and administrators. If first-year teachers become reflective during the beginning of their career, they will soon be among the most effective in your building.

## Build Relationships among Teachers, Coaches, and Administrators

Honest, supportive relationships among teachers, coaches and administrators are not built differently than other relationships. Teachers need to know coaches and administrators are there to support them and that they, too, have student learning as their main focus. This relationship takes time to build but can be destroyed very quickly. Administrators and coaches need to remember not to evaluate, criticize, or divulge any weakness of a teacher to any other teacher. They need to remember that their part of the Shared Classroom Experience is as an equal to the teacher, not as the teacher's evaluator. This is a time to focus on student learning.

## Your Turn  Design Your Own Shared Classroom Experience

Use the contents of this chapter and Reproducible 16, Ten-Step Guide to an Effective Shared Classroom Experience, to design your own Shared Classroom Experience. Reproducibles 17 through 19 are also helpful planning tools.

*"With so many students it's hard to get to every kid and hear their thinking. Having a math coach and a principal in my classroom is a great help; they are extra ears and eyes to see things and hear things from my students that I don't always hear."*

—Kristie Troxell, kindergarten teacher

# Ten-Step Guide to an Effective Shared Classroom Experience

## Before the Lesson

1. Decide participants.

   Who will lead the Shared Classroom Experience (two teachers, same grade level or across grade levels, or a math coach and a teacher)?

   _____

   _____

   Who will be the observers in the Shared Classroom Experience (the principal, math coach, and/or other teachers at the same or different grade levels)?

   _____

   _____

   _____

2. Set the dates and times of each of the four meetings in the Shared Classroom Experience Cycle.

   Meeting 1: Planning the Lesson

   Date:_____     Time:_____     Classroom:_____

   Meeting 2: Briefing Observers

   Date:_____     Time:_____     Classroom:_____

   Meeting 3: Teaching the Lesson

   Date:_____     Time:_____     Classroom:_____

   Meeting 4: Reflecting on the Lesson

   Date:_____     Time:_____     Classroom:_____

3. Hold Meeting 1: Planning the Lesson.

   What are the objectives and student needs?

   _____

   _____

(continued)

Materials needed:

_____

_____

Which teacher will present each part of the lesson?

_____

_____

4. Hold Meeting 2: Briefing Observers. Use Observer Protocol.

## During the Lesson

5. Introduce coteacher and observers to the students.

6. Teach the lesson.

7. Observers listen to student responses, particularly responses that provide evidence of understandings or misconceptions.

8. Gather student artifacts to take to Meeting 4: Reflecting on the Lesson.

## After the Lesson

9. Remind observers of Meeting 4: Reflecting on the Lesson.

10. Hold Meeting 4. Have a conversation about what was seen and learned in the shared classroom. Use Reflective Protocol to guide the conversation.

Experience: _____

_____

_____

_____

_____

_____

_____

_____

_____

_____

# Lesson Planning Tool

1. What is my learning target?

_____
_____
_____
_____
_____
_____
_____

2. What practice problem(s) will go with this objective? What strategy will I utilize for solving the problem(s)?

_____
_____
_____
_____
_____
_____
_____

3. What tools, technology, or other resources will I integrate to increase student engagement?

_____
_____
_____
_____
_____
_____

# Observer Protocol

1. Today, the learning targets for the lesson are: _____

   _____

   _____

   _____

2. The lesson flow includes: _____

   _____

   _____

   _____

   _____

   _____

   _____

   (Sample response: Students sharing prior knowledge about area and
   perimeter; students solving a problem involving area and perimeter,
   sharing solution strategies, and writing a two-minute reflection about
   the learning target)

3. I'm (We're) anticipating students will understand: _____

   _____

   _____

   _____

   _____

   _____

   and might be challenged on _____

   _____

   _____

   _____

   _____

4. I'm (We're) anticipating student strategies for solving the problem might include: _____

_____

_____

_____

_____

_____

_____

5. Strategies to engage students include: _____

_____

_____

_____

_____

_____

6. Comments and/or questions:

# Reflective Protocol

1. Strategies students used to solve the problem include: _____

_____

_____

_____

_____

_____

2. Students seemed to understand: _____

_____

_____

_____

_____

_____

_____

_____

_____

(present evidence—anecdote, student writing, etc.)

3. Students seemed to misunderstand: _____

_____

_____

_____

_____

_____

_____

_____

(present evidence—anecdote, student writing, etc.)

4. Next steps for students who understand include: _____

_____

_____

_____

_____

_____

5. Supports for students misunderstanding include: _____

_____

_____

_____

_____

_____

6. What instructional strategies do we want to add to our professional knowledge base? What worked (e.g., think–pair–share or creating a table)?

_____

_____

_____

_____

_____

7. Comments or questions to push our collective thinking? (What do we need to think about now?)

# Tips for a Successful
# Shared Classroom Experience

1. **Share meeting dates and times in advance.** Make sure that everyone has been informed of the dates for all four meetings (Planning the Lesson, Briefing Observers, Teaching the Lesson, and Reflecting on the Lesson).

2. **Ensure teachers are participating voluntarily in the experience.** If teachers are forced to participate in the Shared Classroom Experience, they will not be open and the learning will not be optimal for teacher or students. If teachers are hesitant, they could be invited to be an observer and work with the coach and administrator so they can see that this experience is truly about student learning. Participants must be open and willing to learn *with* each other.

3. **Support the teachers.** If you are the coach or lead teacher, make sure that you support the teachers in this new experience.

4. **Provide time for planning the lesson.** We have used student teachers, paraprofessionals, and parent volunteers to work with students so teachers have some classroom time to plan. Not having to use their own time helped teachers feel like this time was valued by the principal and was important.

5 **Prepare students for visitors.** The classroom teacher should tell students who will be visiting and what to expect during the lesson.

6. **Invite coteachers and observers to introduce themselves *before* the Shared Classroom Experience.** A few teachers who were going to be visiting stepped in and introduced themselves to the class a few days before the lesson. These teachers reported that students waved to them in the halls for the rest of the year. Getting to know other teachers is particularly important for students. Many students are helped by the security of knowing the adults around them. When these children see the teacher they have next year has taught in their classroom, they feel comfortable because they know the teacher.

7. **Be prompt.** Teachers should not have to wait for observers to arrive; it makes the students and teachers anxious and may affect the outcome of the lesson.

8. **Have observers sit in the back or on the sides of the classroom during direct instruction.** Observers will watch and listen during the direct instruction portion of the lesson, so they should be as inconspicuous as possible.

9. **Encourage observers to engage actively with students during the practice portion of the lesson.** Observers should take an active part in the experience and communicate with the students by asking students questions to discover their thinking processes; this information is vital to the classroom teacher.

10. **Hold Meeting 4: Reflecting on the Lesson in the classroom where the lesson was taught.** This helps freshen participants' memory and allows easy access to student artifacts from the lesson.

11. **Bring artifacts to Meeting 4.** If the meeting is held outside the classroom, the classroom teacher should bring student artifacts from the lesson so they can be discussed.

12. **Keep conversations student focused**. Discuss evidence of student learning or misunderstandings, rather than critique how a lesson was delivered.

13. **Emphasize effectivity.** Shared Classroom Experiences are not to make ineffective teachers into effective teachers but to make effective teachers into more effective teachers.

# Chapter 4

# Mathematics Vertical Learning Team

As schools strive for improvement in student mathematics achievement, developing a strong understanding of how math concepts build from one grade level to the next is essential. A professional learning structure that builds this type of knowledge is the Mathematics Vertical Learning Team. This structure allows teachers, math coaches, teacher leaders, and administrators on the same campus to learn together to deepen their understanding of the learning progressions embedded in the math standards, exploring the sequential nature of math topics and how those topics proceed across the grade levels.

In this chapter, we discuss how such a team is designed for learning and taking action. We

- Offer video clips of a team at work
- Provide step-by-step guidelines for facilitating the meetings
- Share tools: Reproducibles for agendas and for planning the meetings
- Suggest strategies for ensuring successful meetings
- Describe variations to meet different needs

We end the chapter with a "Your Turn" that gives you an opportunity to design your own Mathematics Vertical Learning Team Meeting at the school level.

## Overview

## Tools You Can Use

Videos can be streamed by registering this product at mathsolutions.com/myvideos. See page xxiii for instructions.

Tools You Can Use (Reproducibles) appear at the end of the chapter and are also available online at mathsolutions.com/ givemefivereproducibles.com.

# How It Looks in Practice

At Travis Elementary School, one teacher from each grade level joins the math coach for a Mathematics Vertical Learning Team meeting twice a month. In one meeting, the team's purpose was to reflect on a kindergarten lesson (Racing Bears) designed and implemented using the Common Core Standards for Mathematical Practices, and to explore how the concept of number sense is built across the grades, from addition and subtraction through multiplication and division, and when working with fractions and geometry.

▶ **Video Clip 4.1**

To view this video clip, scan the QR code or access via mathsolutions.com/GMF41

## A Mathematics Vertical Learning Team in Action

As you watch this clip, consider the following questions:

- What stands out for you about the meeting?
- How do you think teachers and students will benefit from the discussion that took place during the meeting?
- Connect this learning experience with ones you've had. How are they similar and different?

Read the authors' reflections on these questions in the Appendix.

**Your Turn** **Defining a Mathematics Vertical Learning Team**

Think about words that come to mind when you hear the term *Mathematics Vertical Learning Team*. Words probably depend on your experiences in participating in a mathematics professional learning community. Consider how a Mathematics Vertical Learning Team could prove useful and productive. List some of the words that come to mind here:

_____

_____

_____

Based on your ideas gleaned from the video clip, write a definition in your own words of a Mathematics Vertical Learning Team.

_____

_____

_____

# What Is a Mathematics Vertical Learning Team?

**The Equation**

Vertical (involving different levels of a progression)

+

Learning (gain or acquire knowledge of or skill in something by study or experience)

+

Team (two or more people working together)

=

Mathematics Success

## The Definition

We define a Mathematics Vertical Learning Team as two or more school-based professionals working together to deepen their knowledge of their state-specific standards and to understand more fully how the learning progressions embedded in those standards support student learning from grade to grade. When the Mathematics Vertical Learning Team collaborates, talk focuses on deepening understanding of content at particular grade levels and how that content builds through the grades. In addition, Mathematics Vertical Learning Teams consider how a particular lesson addresses a standard and how it might be adapted to accommodate students at different points on the learning progression.

### Two Ways to Organize Mathematics Vertical Learning Teams

**K–5 Mathematics Vertical Learning Team.** This team is comprised of one teacher per grade level and a math coach or teacher leader, if possible. One advantage to this team is that it serves as a "curriculum hub" for connecting math content across grade levels and helps ensure coherence through the grades, preventing gaps in the learning progression. The grade-level representatives can then communicate to their grade level using whatever structure the campus or district has in place. The grade level may have a common planning time or it may have grade-level professional learning time (such as Mathematics Content Learning Teams [see Chapter 2]) for the sharing of this information. The math coach may or may not be involved in the grade-level communication.

**K–2 and 3–5 Mathematics Vertical Learning Teams.** These teams are grade-band specific, focusing on content and coherence within their three-year span. Every teacher participates in these learning teams, whereas only one teacher per grade level attends the K–5 sessions. When teams are configured this way, the math coach must be the person who facilitates the cohesion between the teams. The math coach has the privilege of participating with both groups and communicating the conversations and thoughts of each group to the other. If the campus is not too large, both groups could meet together, but the more people who attend, the harder it is for everyone to have a voice. Keep in mind that each grade level needs to be heard at each meeting.

## Research Says . . .

The Common Core State Standards for Mathematics advocate that what and how students are taught should reflect the topics that fall within a certain academic discipline and the key ideas that determine how knowledge is organized and generated within that discipline (National Governors Association Center for Best Practices and Council of Chief State School Officers, 2010 ).

Mike Schmoker (2006) reminds educators that the heart of professional learning communities includes commitments for teachers to meet regularly with their colleagues for two primary purposes: (1) to determine the standards they will teach for student learning in each grade level and (2) to prepare lessons and units together, then assess their impact on student learning.

# Scheduling Mathematics Vertical Learning Teams

Mathematics Vertical Learning Teams meet a minimum of three times per year. Ideally, these teams meet more frequently—one to two times a month, especially after schoolwide benchmark assessment scores are available, so areas of need can be determined schoolwide, and interventions and supports identified. When the team forms at the beginning of the year, one of its first tasks is to set dates and times to meet that are aligned with obtaining school-wide data, and to record the dates on the calendar, which shows commitment to the structure.

# What Is the Agenda for the Mathematics Vertical Learning Team?

The Mathematics Vertical Learning Team structure provides a time and space for professionals to learn together with a common purpose and focus: to deepen their understanding of content learning progressions across the grade levels, to understand the mathematical practices teachers should develop in their students (as identified in their standards), and to enact and revise lessons based on the standards. Meeting agendas might look like this:

| Meeting 1: Launching the Mathematics Vertical Learning Team | Meetings 2, 3, and Beyond: Learning Together in the Mathematics Vertical Learning Team |
|---|---|
| Step 1: What is the focus? | Step 1: Are we all connected? |
| Step 2: How do we ensure we stay focused? | Step 2: What learning progression do we need to learn about more? |
| Step 3: What are our roles and what is the agenda? | Step 3: What have we learned and what are our next steps? |

*"The Mathematics Vertical Learning Team really helped to broaden my understanding of math and get the whole picture. When I first started teaching, I was just studying fifth-grade curriculum, but it's so important to have the big picture of all elementary grade levels and to be able to know what questions to ask."*

—Erin Easley, fifth-grade teacher

## Meeting 1 Launching the Mathematics Vertical Learning Team

**Approximate Time**   60 minutes

**Scheduling**   This meeting happens early during the school year.

**Objectives**
- Establish expectations and set the tone for the year.
- Establish norms and begin team building.
- Set and communicate purpose and goals to participants.
- Clarify roles and responsibilities.
- Create a Learning Agenda to promote discussion and inquiry.

| Step | Documents to Revisit or Create |
|------|-------------------------------|
| Step 1:  What is the focus? | Action Plan: revisit (from Chapter 1) |
| Step 2:  How do we ensure we stay focused? | Norms for Behavior and Learning: revisit (from Chapter 1) |
| Step 3:  What are our roles and what is the agenda? | Roles and Responsibilities Chart: create |
| | Learning Agenda: create |

## Step 1: **What Is the Focus?** (10–20 minutes)

*Objective: Establish expectations and set the tone for the year*

Much like the Mathematics Content Learning Team (see Chapter 2), the first meeting establishes expectations and sets the tone for the year. The math coach or other math teacher leader facilitates this first meeting. If the school's Action Plan (see Chapter 1) has set a focus for the Mathematics Vertical Learning Team, the facilitator communicates it to participants. Otherwise, turn to data to determine areas of need.

It is important to distinguish the difference between the purpose of the Mathematics Content Learning Team and the purpose of the Mathematics Vertical Learning Team. The Mathematics Content Learning Team focuses conversations on grade-level mathematics, allowing teachers an opportunity to deepen their understanding of the math in the standards. Guiding questions include: What is the math students should learn? What knowledge do we need to design lessons for students to learn the math? Mathematics Vertical Learning Teams, on the other hand, address math progressions across the grade levels, and topics are determined by data. For example, when longitudinal data indicate the lowest test scores are in the fraction domain, then teachers study the fraction progression across the grades to ensure there are no gaps for students. Guiding questions for the Mathematics Vertical Learning Teams include: What is the math with which students struggle across the grades? What should students know and be able to do at each grade level? What should we do to ensure students master the important standards at each grade level? What should we do if students have a "gap?"

> **Key Questions**
> - What does the data say about our students' mathematical learning needs?
> - What are the related standards?
> - How can we better understand the content and how it develops across grade levels so we can design more effective lessons for students?

**Key Questions**

- How do we ensure our time together is meaningful, valuable, and relevant to our classroom practice?
- How are we going to ensure that we stay focused to learn how to support students?

## Step 2: How Do We Ensure We Stay Focused? (10–20 minutes)

*Objective:  Establish norms and begin team building*

The designated facilitator establishes norms for group learning using the protocol described in detail in Chapter 1 (see page 58). If participants are familiar with the idea of norms and have adopted a set in another situation, a brief review of them and commitment to them will suffice.

### Seven Norms of Collaboration

1. Pausing
2. Paraphrasing
3. Putting Inquiry at the Center
4. Probing for Specificity

5. Putting Ideas on the Table
6. Paying Attention to Self and Others
7. Presuming Positive Intentions

*Source:* Garmston and Wellman (2009). See Chapter 1 for a full discussion and protocol for introducing norms to learning teams.

**Key Questions**

- How can we make our meetings run smoothly?
- How can we structure our meetings to keep focused on the math learning?

Refer to Reproducibles 22 and 23 when planning the Learning Agenda for each meeting.

## Step 3: What Are Our Roles and What Is the Agenda? (20 minutes)

*Objective:  Clarify roles and responsibilites*

For meetings to run smoothly for groups of more than four people, it is helpful to assign various roles so it is clear who is responsible for key tasks. Table 4–1 on the next page shows examples of roles that larger teams have used. During the initial meeting, the team creates a chart outlining the responsibilities of each role and makes a rotation schedule so it's clear who will fulfill which role for each meeting. The schedule should be emailed to all participants.

In addition, share Reproducible 22, the Meeting 1 Agenda and Reproducible 23, Meeting 2 and Beyond Agenda, which facilitators will use to plan the Learning Agenda for each meeting. Topics for conversation originate from data sources, such as schoolwide test data or quarterly benchmark data. Discuss the organization of the agendas and how they can be used to guide meetings. As with the Mathematics Content Learning Teams, we recommend all team roles rotate among team members.

**TABLE 4–1. Roles and Responsibilities for Mathematics Vertical Learning Teams of Four or More People**

| Roles | Responsibilities |
|---|---|
| Facilitator | • Prepares the Learning Agenda and emails it at least two days before the meeting, along with reminders about items to bring and actions to take. |
| | • Starts and ends the meeting on time. |
| | • Facilitates team building. |
| | • Leads participants through the Learning Agenda. |
| | • Encourages members to participate. |
| | • Keeps talk focused on mathematics learning, referring to norms as necessary. |
| | • Summarizes the one to three points of learning the group wants to remember and the actions participants will take before the next meeting. |
| Recorder | • Documents the points of learning. |
| | • Documents the actions participants agree to take before the next meeting. |
| | • Reminds participants of the roles they have for the next meeting. |
| | • Emails participants all this information as soon as possible after the meeting. |
| Timekeeper | • Watches the time and cues the facilitator if any step is running longer than planned. |
| | • Alerts the facilitator when there are five minutes left so the team can summarize the learning and plan the actions to take for the next meeting. |
| Team Member (everyone at the meeting) | • Comes prepared to the meeting. |
| | • Participates actively in the meeting. |
| | • Stays focused on the Learning Agenda. |

**Meeting 2** **Learning Together in the Mathematics Vertical Learning Team**

**Approximate Time**   60 minutes

**Scheduling**   Meetings happen at least three times a year; ideally, they occur biweekly throughout the school year.

**Objectives**

- Create a team-building environment.
- Understand the math learning progression that underlies the state standards.
- Articulate learning points and actions.

| Step | Documents to Revisit, Preselect, or Create |
|------|---------------------------------------------|
| Step 1:  Are we all connected? | |
| Step 2:  What learning progression do we need to learn about more? | Learning Agenda: preselect |
| Step 3:  What have we learned and what are our next steps? | Points of Learning: create |
| | Actions: create |

**Key Questions**

- What do we need to understand about each other before the meeting starts?
- Is anyone attending who has not attended previously?

## Step 1:  Are We All Connected? (5 minutes)

*Objective:  Create a team-building environment*

Each meeting should begin with a few minutes of conversation to help team members connect socially and transition from the fast school pace to a slower learning pace, so everyone can be completely and fully present during the learning conversations. The facilitator may review the norms and ask if everyone can adhere to them, reminding participants that if the norms are not being followed, anyone in the group should feel comfortable in saying, "Remember the norms." If something out of the ordinary has happened at school or even in the world that day, it may need to be addressed before the meeting begins.

## Step 2: What Learning Progression Do We Need to Learn about More? (50 minutes)

*Objective: Understand the math learning progression that underlies the state standards*

The Learning Agenda is the heart of the meeting and provides a structure for collaborative learning. The agenda differs based on whether the team is focusing on the mathematics learning progression (Reproducible 22, Meeting Agenda 1) or lesson design (Reproducible 23, Meeting Agenda 2).

### Meeting Agenda 1:
### Studying the Learning Progression in Standards

1. *Share actions taken, results, and conclusions about the action.* (10 minutes) Each person shares the outcome of an action taken after the previous meeting, and shares evidence, such as student work samples of exit tickets.

2. *Identify content standard currently under study.* (10 minutes) Name the standard currently under study. For example, if data indicate that students struggle with multiplying and dividing within one hundred fluently and with solving problems using the four operations, especially multiplication and division, a team may focus on Operations and Algebraic Thinking, examining how it progresses across the grade levels.

3. *Determine which mathematics practices students need to develop to meet the standard.* (20 minutes) Next, the team considers the Big Ideas students need to know at each grade level for this standard. Teachers divide up the work by grade level. Each teacher or grade-level team studies their grade-level standard, then writes the Big Ideas on a poster. Display the posters in order on the wall or whiteboard, creating a visual of the Operations and Algebraic Thinking progression from kindergarten to fifth grade.

4. *Document how the math ideas connect from one grade level to another.* (10 minutes) As teachers look across the grade levels, they identify key changes from grade to grade. For Operations and Algebraic Thinking, kindergarten children need to develop a sophisticated level of counting, understanding counting on and reasoning to count a set of objects. First- and second-grade students learn to structure numbers in groups, count by groups, and develop three methods for solving problems: direct modeling, counting on, and converting to an easier problem. Third-grade students need to do more than "memorize

**Key Questions**
- What is the Big Idea Flow across the standards?
- How do we design a lesson aligned to the standards?
- How do we design a lesson to develop mathematical practices in students?

See How to Build a Big Idea Flow in Chapter 2 (page 112).

See Reproducible 24, Guide to Understanding Vertical Progressions in Common Core State Standards for Mathematics.

their facts"; they needed to develop a conceptual understanding of multiplication and division, and know how to use the operations in different problem-solving situations that are either one- or multistep situations. Fourth- and fifth-grade students begin to use more abstract symbols, larger numbers, develop formal algorithms and procedures, and use properties of operations more frequently.

### Meeting Agenda 2:
### Designing, Teaching, Revising, and Connecting Lessons to Standards

1. *Share actions taken, results, and conclusions about the action.*
   (10 minutes)  Each person shares the outcome of an action taken after the previous meeting, and shares evidence, such as students work samples of exit tickets.

2. *Discuss math lesson being designed or discuss how a math lesson was taught, considering ways to revise for better implementation next time.*
   (20 minutes)  Teachers can present a math lesson they've designed and plan to teach, eliciting feedback and suggestions from the group. Teachers may also share how a lesson went in the classroom, reflecting on the experience, analyzing student work samples, and considering changes that might improve the lesson next time. For example, when debriefing a lesson on fractions, fourth-grade teachers noticed that more than half of students had difficulty comparing fractions. After discussion, the teachers revised the lesson to increase the use of visuals and representations to demonstrate equivalency.

3. *Explore how the math in the lesson connects across grade levels.*
   (20 minutes)  Now teachers consider how the math concepts and challenges might play out in other grade levels. For example, because fourth-graders frequently guessed when comparing fractions such as six-eighths and three-fourths or two-thirds and three-fourths, teachers looked back at the third-grade tasks related to the standard and realized students must be able to explain equivalence and compare fractions by reasoning about their size (CCSS.MATH.CONTENT.3.NF.A3) before they can extend their understanding of fraction equivalence and ordering. Third-grade teachers agreed to investigate how their students were performing on that standard, and the fourth-grade teachers determined to plan lessons and activities to review CCSS.MATH.CONTENT.3.NF.A.3.B "Recognize and generate simple equivalent fractions."

## Step 3: What Have We Learned and What Are Our Next Steps? (5 minutes)

**Key Questions**
- What actions will we take next?
- What evidence will we bring to the next meeting?

*Objective: Articulate learning points and actions*

When there are five minutes left in the meeting, the timekeeper signals the facilitator, who then wraps up the discussion and prompts participants to articulate one to three points of learning they want to remember. The recorder documents these points and emails them to participants after the meeting.

Finally, the facilitator asks participants which actions they will commit to doing before the next meeting. We recommend naming one to three actions related to the Learning Agenda. For example, for one team, as a result of the Mathematics Vertical Learning Team conversations, two actions were taken:

1. Each grade level chose an assessment task to administer to their students. The tasks were aligned with standards that progressed across the grade levels in the fraction strand: K.CC.B.4.C, Understand that each successive number name refers to a quantity that is one larger; 1.G.A.3, Partition circles and rectangles into two and four equal shares, describe the shares using the words *halves, fourths,* and *quarters,* and use the phrases *half of, fourth of,* and *quarter of*; 2.G.A.3, Partition circles and rectangles into two, three, or four equal shares, describe the shares using the words *halves, thirds, half of, a third of,* etc., and describe the whole as two halves, three thirds, four fourths; 3.NF.A.3, Explain equivalence of fractions in special cases, and compare fractions by reasoning about their size; 4.NF.A.1, Explain why a fraction $a/b$ is equivalent to a fraction $(n \times a)/(n \times b)$ by using visual fraction models, with attention to how the number and size of the parts differ even though the two fractions themselves are the same size. Use this principle to recognize and generate equivalent fractions; and 5.NF.A.1, Add and subtract fractions with unlike denominators.

2. All grade teachers agreed to administer the task to their students and to bring back student work samples to assess student understanding collaboratively.

Participants will begin the next meeting by reporting on the results of these actions and analyzing the data. The recorder will note these actions and include them in the email along with the learning points.

**Video Clip 4.2**

To view this video clip, scan the QR code or access via mathsolutions.com/GMF42

## Building Knowledge in a Mathematics Vertical Learning Team

In this clip, the Mathematics Vertical Learning Team at Travis Elementary reflects on the kindergarten Racing Bears lesson and explores how number sense builds across the grades. Watch for when teachers share the points of learning they want to remember. While you watch, consider these questions:

- Which instructional strategies from the lesson do the teachers value and decide to use in their own teaching?
- What other kinds of ideas were shared that can affect teachers' practice?
- How does this type of discussion lead to improved mathematics instruction?

See the authors' reflections on these questions in the Appendix.

## It Can Really Happen . . . Insights from the Field

Three years in a row, the lowest scores on state math assessments at Westfield Elementary were in the fraction domain. Teachers and school administrators kept wondering why scores dropped from third, to fourth, to fifth each year, and plateaued from year to year. It seemed that whatever teachers were doing to improve students' conceptual and procedural understanding of fractions wasn't working. Teachers were working so hard, and not seeing students improve. With the purchase of new textbooks and new resources designed to increase student understanding of fractions, it was hoped that test scores and student understanding of fractions would improve. The new math coach suggested that if each grade level understood its role in students' mastery of standards leading to proficiency with fractions, then students may be better supported. The school formed a Mathematics Vertical Learning Team that studied the vertical progression of fraction standards across the grades. The team learned there was a K–2 pathway that develops students' conceptual readiness for formal study of fractions, yet the pathway was not visible when teachers read the standards. For example, the Number and Operations–Fraction Domain begins in the standards in grade 3. Teachers in grades K–2 assumed students didn't learn fractions until grade 3, because there was not a fraction domain in K–2. However, when the Mathematics Vertical Learning Team studied the standards, they learned that students in grades K–2 develop fraction concepts informally in the geometry domain, which specifies students learn about fair and equal shares, and understand halves and quarters with shapes. The third-grade teacher discovered that students develop fraction concepts formally, and fourth- and fifth-grade teachers support students learning formal operations with fractions. The Mathematics Vertical Learning Team discovered that students can't wait to develop fraction understanding until third grade; it starts in K–2, even though not stated explicitly in the standards. They learned that third-grade teachers develop concepts, not procedures, and that if fourth- and fifth-grade students have a deep conceptual understanding of fractions, then they are more likely to be successful with learning formal procedures. The following year, scores increased as teachers in the Mathematics Vertical Learning Team invested time in studying the standards vertically.

## The Framework for a Mathematics Vertical Learning Team
### Before the meeting, the facilitator . . .

1. *Identifies the purpose for learning.* The purpose may be to study research-based learning progressions to understand more completely how students' mathematical knowledge and skill develops over time, then examine the progression embedded in state standards. Or, the purpose may be to design a lesson to teach a particular standard, discuss its implementation, then revise and reteach as necessary.

2. *Sets the Learning Agenda.* If the focus is on learning progressions, Reproducible 22, Meeting Agenda 1 can be used to guide the meeting. If the focus is on lesson design, Reproducible 23, Meeting Agenda 2 can be used to guide the meeting.

3. *Gathers/requests necessary materials.* The facilitator gathers materials the team will need, which may include copies of the standards for mathematics, standards-based lessons, or professional resources (such as journal articles or curriculum maps).

4. *Determines roles and responsibilities.* Identify who will fulfill what role during the meeting, according to a rotating schedule. Roles include facilitator, recorder, and timekeeper (refer back to Table 4-1); all participants are expected to be active team members.

See Reproducibles 22 and 23 to set the learning agendas.

*(continued)*

**The Framework for a Mathematics Vertical Learning Team** *(continued)*

**During the meeting, participants . . .**

5. *Participate in team building.* Spend a few minutes reconnecting with team members and getting in the professional learning mindset. Review norms for learning , if necessary.

6. *Focus the discussion on math, following the appropriate Learning Agenda.* Share the actions and results from last time, then move on to the meeting's current focus for learning.

7. *Document the learning and identify next steps.* Articulate points of learning the group would like to remember; the recorder documents these. Then, identify next steps—the actions each member will take to improve math achievement in his or her classroom; the recorder documents these as well. All notes will be emailed to participants.

**After the meeting, participants . . .**

8. *Take action.* Each participant carries out the action agreed to at the meeting.

9. *Collect and analyze results.* Each participant documents the results of the action through anecdotal notes and/or student work, then analyzes the results.

10. *Prepare to share and discuss actions and results at the next meeting.* Each participant prepares a story to tell about the action taken and the results seen.

### Tips for Being Prepared for a Meeting

Email participants two to three days before the meeting with materials requests, a copy of the agenda, and a reminder about the actions to which the group agreed at the last meeting. Also, include information about who is fulfilling the roles of facilitator, recorder, and timekeeper, as these roles alternate.

See also Reproducible 25, Tips for a Successful Mathematics Vertical Learning Team Meeting.

## Strategies for Success

Many of the strategies shared for the Mathematics Content Learning Teams (see Chapter 2, page 118) apply to Mathematics Vertical Learning Teams, including

- Keep focused on the agenda
- Plan for unprepared participants
- Encourage full participation
- Probe for specifics

In addition, consider the following strategies specific to Mathematics Vertical Learning Teams.

## Use Lesson Design to Close the Knowing–Teaching Gap

Research shows us there is a knowing and doing gap; knowledge of something doesn't always mean that knowledge can be translated into action (Reeves 2006, Pfeffer and Sutton 2000). It's one thing to study and understand a concept or strategy, but it's quite another to put it into practice in the classroom. We often hear teachers say "it's just too hard to find time to learn all the new things 'they' [district administrators, state policymakers] require us to do." Mathematics Vertical Learning Team meetings allow time for teachers to engage in professional talk about how math progresses across the grade levels, and how specific lessons can be designed for all students to access the standards. As teachers plan lessons, teach them, and then share results with each other, they are putting ideas into practice and learning from them in a way that affects student achievement positively.

## Link Lessons to Standards

From an experienced teacher's perspective, finding time to learn about new standards or understand the mathematics learning progression while continuing to manage day-to-day teaching tasks focused on student learning requires intensive time, effort, energy, and focus. From a math coach or teacher leader's perspective, finding time to meet with teachers and focus on new and rigorous standards is challenging at best. The Mathematics Vertical Learning Team structure provides time for teachers, math coaches, and teacher leaders to slow down, communicate, collaborate, and connect to each other as they design standards-based lessons and discuss their implementation. The double benefit is deepening understanding of the standards while creating practical lessons with the support and companionship of other educators.

## Adapt a Lesson to Different Grade Levels

A Mathematics Vertical Learning Team structure provides time during the school day for teachers, teacher leaders, and math coaches to think deeply and carefully about how a lesson designed around their standards gets put into practice, and how the content ideas follow one another across the grade levels. After a lesson has been taught, evaluated, and revised at one grade level, a useful exercise is to consider how that classroom-tested lesson can be adapted to meet the needs of students at different stages of the learning progression for that standard. This can help teachers differentiate instruction for students of different levels in their own classroom and serves as a resource for teachers in other grade levels as they prepare to teach the same standard, but at their level on the learning progression.

## A Mathematics Vertical Learning Team in Action, Revisited

Rewatch Video Clip 4.1 and consider these questions:

- Which connections does the fourth-grade teacher make to the math in the kindergarten lesson?
- How can these types of conversations lead to improved student learning?
- What is a lesson you could share in a Mathematics Vertical Learning Team meeting that would be helpful to adapt to different grade levels?

See the authors' reflections on these questions in the Appendix.

To view this video clip, scan the QR code or access via mathsolutions.com/ GMF41

## Research Says . . .

The need for Mathematics Vertical Learning Teams is clear. Research informs us that widespread agreement exists that teachers need improved mathematics knowledge for teaching (Hill and Ball 2004).

The Common Core State Standards for Mathematics strives toward greater focus and coherence in mathematical instruction not only by stressing conceptual understanding of key ideas, but also by returning continually to organizing principles such as place value or the laws of arithmetic to structure those ideas (National Governors Association Center for Best Practices & Council of Chief State School Officers 2010).

**Your Turn** | **Design Your Own Mathematics Vertical Learning Team Meeting**

Use Reproducible 21, Ten-Step Guide to an Effective Mathematics Vertical Learning Team Meeting, Reproducible 22, Meeting 1 Agenda (Key Questions), and Reproducible 23, Meeting 2 Agenda to design your own Mathematics Vertical Learning Team Meeting.

# Ten-Step Guide to an Effective Mathematics Vertical Learning Team Meeting

## Before the Meeting

1. **Purpose:** Identify the purpose. Study research-based learning progressions to better understand how students' mathematical knowledge and skill develops over time.

2. **Learning Agenda:** Create the agenda.

3. **Resources:** Gather necessary resources (Common Core State Standards or other state-specific standards for mathematics and lessons designed using Common Core or state-specific standards).

4. **Roles and Responsibilities:** Clarify roles and responsibilities (facilitator, timekeeper, recorder, and member).

## During the Meeting

5. **Establish Norms:** Set norms for learning and behavior (do this in the very first meeting). For all meetings after the first one, begin with actions taken from the previous meeting.

6. **Learning Progression Specific:** Focus talk on Common Core State Standards or other state-specific standards learning progressions.

7. **Learning Points and Actions:** Identify and document learning and action steps.

## After the Meeting

8. **Actions:** Act on next steps.

9. **Evidence:** Document evidence of taking action on next step.

10. **Share:** Identify evidence to take to the next Mathematics Vertical Learning Team meeting.

## Mathematics Vertical Learning Team

# Meeting 1 Agenda
# (Key Questions)

This protocol is designed to be used when any Mathematics Vertical Learning Team meets for the first time to learn together in a community.

1. **Introduction:** Who's in the room? How is everyone? (5 minutes)

2. **Norms:** What norms will help us learn together? (5 minutes)

3. **Purpose:** What is the purpose of our work together? (10 minutes)
   - Deepen knowledge of Common Core State Standards (content learning progressions and mathematical practices).
   - Design, enact, and revise lessons to develop student understanding.
   - Assess student understanding.

4. **Roles and Responsibilities:** What are our roles and responsibilities? (5 minutes)

   *Facilitator* (rotates each session)
   - Creates the learning agenda
   - Uses norms to keep the conversation focused on agenda
   - Designates next session's facilitator

   *Recorder*
   - Documents learning and next steps
   - Designates next session's facilitator

   *Group Member*
   - Attends fully to conversation

   *Timekeeper*
   - Keeps track of time and informs facilitator

5. **Data:** What does data say? (15 minutes)
   - Use data sources (state assessments, benchmark) to identify what students know and demonstrate they can do

*(continued)*

6. **Standards:**  How do we study vertical articulation using Common Core or state specific standards? (10 minutes)

   - Use Common Core or state-specific standards to study the design and framework so everyone develops common language and understanding about how to read and use the standards.

   - Identify the mathematical practices to develop for students.

7. **Reflection:**  What did we learn today? (5 minutes)

   - Reflect on content and process

     **Content:**

     Facilitator asks group to identify one to three points of learning to try in practice before the next team session (things to remember and try).

     Facilitator documents learning on one-pager.

     Facilitator documents next steps (things "to do" in practice and reflect on for next session).

     **Process:**

     What was the best part/most challenging part of the meeting?

8. **Looking Forward:**  What are our next steps? (5 minutes)

   - What evidence will I bring to the next meeting?

   - When is the next meeting?

# Meeting 2 Agenda
# (Key Questions)

The following questions can be used to design a Mathematics Vertical Learning Team agenda for the second meeting and beyond. Questions are used as a framework for creating agendas for meetings during the year.

1. **Introduction:** Who's in the room? How is everyone? (5 minutes)

2. **Actions:** What actions did you take from the last meeting? (5 minutes)
   Each person shares what action was taken and the result.

3. **Progressions-Specific:** Agendas after the first ten minutes depend on each team's purpose and focus. Teams will use some of the questions (not all depending on focus). (35 minutes)
   Here are some sample questions for team agendas:
   - What does data say?
   - What is the mathematics content identified in the Common Core or state-specific standards across the grades?
   - What are the mathematical practices to develop in students?
   - What are the content learning progressions across the standards?
   - How do we design a lesson aligned to Common Core content?
   - How do we design a lesson to develop mathematical practices in students?
   - What lesson do we want to share today?

4. **Reflection:** What did we learn? (5 minutes)
   - Document one to three actions to remember.

5. **Looking Ahead:** What actions do we take? (5 minutes)
   - What are our next steps?
   - When is the next meeting?

# Guide to Understanding the Vertical Progressions in Common Core State Standards for Mathematics

A progression describes a sequence of increasing complexity in understanding of concepts and skills in an area of study. Several types of progressions are embedded in the Common Core State Standards for Mathematical Practice:

1. Domain Progression

   Here is how the domains are distributed across the Common Core State Standards:

   | | |
   |---|---|
   | K | Counting and Cardinality |
   | K–5 | Numbers and Operations: Base 10 |
   | 3–5 | Numbers and Operations: Fractions |
   | K–5 | Numbers and Algebraic Thinking |
   | K–5 | Geometry |
   | K–5 | Measurement and Data |

2. Learning Progression

   A learning progression refers to how a math idea develops over time.

   *Example:*  Learning Progression for Place Value: The Role of Counting

   | | |
   |---|---|
   | *Unitary:* | Count by ones approach |
   | *Base ten:* | Groups of ten approach |
   | *Equivalent:* | Nonstandard base ten approach |

3. Standards Progression

   The standards progression refers to how the written standards progress across grade levels.

   For fractions, the standards progression is

   • Develop an understanding of fractions as numbers

   • Extend understanding of fraction equivalence and ordering

   • Build fractions from unit fractions by applying and extending previous understandings of operations on whole numbers

   • Understand decimal notation for fractions and compare decimal fractions

   • Use equivalent fractions as a strategy to add and subtract fractions

   • Apply and extend previous understandings of multiplication and division to multiply and divide fractions.

   • Apply and extend previous understandings of multiplication and division to divide fractions by fractions

4. Task Progression

   Task progression refers to a rich task that is organized to serve different mathematical goals and for students' access to the mathematics in the problem

   *Example:* Number Balances Problem

   This problem features the following progression of skills:

   - Developing the concept of a balance
   - Making a representation of a balance
   - Identifying place value using tools (base ten blocks)
   - Solving number puzzles with increasing complexity
   - Using addition and subtraction strategies
   - Designing number puzzles

# Tips for a Successful
# Mathematics Vertical Learning Team Meeting

1. **Do make small talk.** Human connections during the first few minutes of a meeting are not wasted time; they put us in touch with each other.

2. **Start and end on time.** Try passing out a small reward (like a pen or pad of sticky notes) to everyone who is present at the appointed time.

3. **Post agreed-to learning and behavior norms in the meeting space for easy reference.**

4. **Post the mathematical progression to center the conversation around content.** This makes it easier for teachers to see the steps leading to a skill or concept that could create a gap that might need future differentiation.

5. **Encourage the sharing of resources.** There may be a second-grade student who needs the counting beans that are used in kindergarten, but the second-grade teacher may have no idea these manipulatives exist; this is the time to share with each other.

6. **Encourage the principal to attend team meetings.** His or her presence at these meetings ensures they are seen as important to student learning and are taken seriously.

7. **Have clear roles.** Roles include facilitator, member, time-keeper, and recorder.

8. **Rotate roles.** Role rotation ensures that leadership is distributed and the meeting is not dependent on one person.

9. **Learn to appreciate teachers in other grade levels.** Often, teachers are focused on their grade level and don't get the opportunity to see where a skill begins or how it develops. Understanding the arc of a skill and how it looks at different grade levels helps teachers appreciate each other and makes the team stronger.

10. **Connect to the classroom.** Ensure talk is relevant and authentic to current student learning.

11. **Share with teachers who are not in attendance.** Remind grade-level representatives that they are responsible for sharing knowledge and insights from the Mathematics Vertical Learning Team with their grade level.

12. **Use the standards.** Be a place to deepen understanding of Common Core State Standards or other state-specific standards across the grade levels.

13. **Use evidence.** Include taking actions with students and sharing results (for example, one to two things to do, learn from, record results, and share at the next meeting).

14. **Use a Parking Lot.** "Park" issues that need more time for conversation. These issues can be addressed at the beginning of the next meeting.

15. **Keep it positive.** Know how to engage in healthy, professional disagreements about ideas, not people and have at least one agreed upon strategy for dealing with passionate disagreements.

16. **Celebrate!** Do something enjoyable to mark occasions of success, learning, and perseverance!

# Chapter 5

# Ten-Minute Meeting

Collaborative school cultures and creativity in teaching linked to supporting student learning arise from interactions among people. Educators need to collaborate to create a shared language, develop a common understanding of teaching and learning, and build the trust and rapport required for members of a group to suggest original and untried solutions. Opportunities to work on these crucial factors are not readily available across a school during the day, or among professionals with different roles and status levels. Educators at all levels feel as if there is no extra time to be had in the school day, and often teachers feel that it's challenging to talk with administrators. The Ten-Minute Meeting collaboration structure makes it possible for everyone to find time to talk; it also levels the playing field in a hierarchical top-down system, and allows everyone to get on the same page.

In this chapter, we discuss how such a meeting is designed for effective communication and collaboration. We

- Offer video clips showing excerpts from a meeting
- Provide step-by-step guidelines for facilitating meetings
- Share tools: Reproducibles for agendas and for planning meetings
- Suggest strategies for ensuring successful meetings

We end the chapter with a "Your Turn" that gives you an opportunity to design your own Ten-Minute Meeting.

## Overview

## Tools You Can Use

Videos can be streamed by registering this product at mathsolutions.com/myvideos. See page xxiii for more info.

Tools You Can Use (Reproducibles) appear at the end of the chapter and are also available online at mathsolutions.com/givemefivereproducibles.

# How It Looks in Practice

Ms. Cory, the math coach at Lamar Elementary, faces an intensely exciting yet daunting role on her campus of 650 students. She has been asked to support both teacher and student learning on a daily basis. Looking ahead to the new school year, Ms. Cory's dilemma is to define her role clearly so she can be the most effective coach possible, given all the additional responsibilities she has accumulated. Ms. Cory requests a Ten-Minute Meeting with the principal, Ms. Cleek, to clarify her role and responsibilities to ensure the principal and she share the same understanding of how things will proceed next year.

▶ **Video Clip 5.1**

To view this video clip, scan the QR code or access via mathsolutions.com/GMF51

## A Ten-Minute Meeting in Action

As you watch this clip between the principal Ms. Cleek and the math coach Ms. Cory, consider the following questions:

- What stands out for you about the meeting?
- Did the meeting seem like a productive use of time? Why or why not?
- How does this meeting compare with those you have had with key personnel in your building or district?

See the authors' reflections on these questions in the Appendix.

**Your Turn**   Defining a Ten-Minute Meeting

Think about words that come to mind when you hear the term *Ten-Minute Meeting*. Words probably depend on your experiences with meetings. Consider how a Ten-Minute Meeting could be useful and productive. List some of the words that come to mind here:

_____

_____

_____

Based on your ideas gleaned from the video clip, write a definition in your own words of a Ten-Minute Meeting.

_____

_____

_____

_____

_____

# What Is a Ten-Minute Meeting?

## The Equation

Ten minutes (period of time equal to 600 seconds)

**+**

Meeting (assembling for a particular purpose)

**=**

Mathematics Success

## The Definition

We define a Ten-Minute Meeting as a structured event that occurs when two or more school-based professionals—such as a math coach and principal, or teacher, principal, and teacher leader—convene for ten minutes to discuss no more than three purposeful questions that get at the heart of a key issue. As educators meet, either in person or via technology such as a conference call, they work to get everyone on the same page, using the same language and having the same response in regard to the questions. With the dizzying pace of the school day, educators and administrators often feel there's no time to meet. However, meeting for ten minutes is doable, and this type of short, focused collaborative meeting is essential for defining roles, clarifying tasks, realizing goals, addressing misconceptions, and preventing confusion.

## Research Says . . .

During her time as Vice President of Google Product Search Google, Marissa Mayer held about seventy short meetings a week. Much of her work with eight teams of managers, directors, and engineers took place in meetings, and the goal was to ensure everyone had actionable information, clear expectations, and a strategic direction (Gallo 2006). Even five-minute meetings had a clear agenda.

The Springfield Education Association reports on their website that "10 minute meetings are a great communication tool to quickly convey information to our fabulous members" (Springfield Education Association 2011).

# Scheduling Ten-Minute Meetings

Ten-Minute Meetings happen whenever there is a need for someone to have clarity on a topic, issue, or task. The meeting is scheduled any time that is convenient and agreed on by all persons involved, before, during, or after school. The meeting is initiated by the person who has questions that must be addressed to continue moving forward with some element of the school's Vision Statement or Action Plan (see Chapter 1). This person creates one to three questions that will provide clarity on the issue and allow forward momentum to continue. The key is to use time, not to spend time.

At the start of the school year, considerable time is spent in goal setting for change, as described in Chapter 1. Goals are often linked to state test results ("We've got to raise scores or keep them high") and are accompanied by changes in administration and/or staffing, along with the introduction of new initiatives. Everyone is either excited about the possibilities for change and improvement ("Yes! Things should get better now."), apprehensive as a result of new administration ("I wonder if the new principal will have her own agenda?"), or skeptical that this is yet another year of more of the same ("Yeah, right. All talk; no action."). The new school year brings anticipation, expectations, and excitement.

After the school year gets underway, the day-to-day routine is fast paced, and it's easy to lose sight of even the most well-intentioned and carefully crafted goals. Ten-Minute Meetings serve as a pause point and we recommend holding them early in the year to ensure each teacher, principal, math coach, and teacher leader's actions and behaviors are aligned with the school's goals and are moving in the same direction. This minimizes human frustration and ambiguity, and maximizes clarity about what to do. In addition, these meetings can be used throughout the year to clarify roles and responsibilities, address specific problems that arise, and check in about progress toward goals. It is easy to get off course—to get distracted from intended goals—with the whirl-wind pace of the school day. Setting aside ten minutes for focused conversation resets the course toward intended outcomes and promotes confidence and hope that goals can be realized.

# What Is the Agenda for the Ten-Minute Meeting?

Each Ten-Minute Meeting has a different focus, but it is always linked to issues that need to be clarified. Most important, the meeting is preplanned—designed to be structured, productive, and hopeful. To this end, we discuss three phases that make up the meeting:

| Phase 1: Planning the Ten-Minute Meeting | Phase 2: Facilitating the Ten-Minute Meeting | Phase 3: Following Up |
|---|---|---|
| Step 1: What is the issue? | Step 1: How can we best set the tone? | Step 1: What response did we reach for each question? |
| Step 2: What are the key questions? | Step 2: What are the questions we have? | Step 2: What did we agree to? |
| Step 3: When is the meeting? | Step 3: Have we reached a common understanding? | Step 3: What are the next steps? |

## Phase 1    Planning the Ten-Minute Meeting

**Approximate Time**    10 minutes

**Scheduling**    Planning occurs as soon as an issue arises.

**Objectives**

- Identify the issue.
- Develop key questions that will bring clarity to the issue.
- Determine who will participate, then schedule a meeting.

**Give Me Five!**

| Step | Document to Create |
|---|---|
| Step 1: What is the issue? | |
| Step 2: What are the key questions? | Three Questions |
| Step 3: When is the meeting? | |

## Step 1:  **What Is the Issue?** (2–3 minutes)

*Objective:  **Identify the issue***

As soon as a problem or confusion arises, the educator or administrator should think through and identify the source of the issue in preparation for initiating a Ten-Minute Meeting. For example, the second-grade team at Wilson Elementary decided to plan a ten-minute meeting with the math coach and district curriculum director to clarify how to use the textbook to plan lessons. The teachers were getting mixed messages about what to consider when planning math lessons. They had a district curriculum map, a textbook, and state standards; they understood the standards came first, yet they received a district message saying to "use the textbook with fidelity" and to use the curriculum map for pacing. The teachers understood they were to be on the same page on the same day, but they had questions: What if students didn't master the standard? Could they slow the pace? How do they connect the three different resources? What do they consider first when planning: standards, curriculum map, or textbook?

## Step 2:  **What Are the Key Questions?** (5–10 minutes)

*Objective:  **Develop key questions that will bring clarity to the issue***

Next, the meeting initiator should develop one to three questions to help concerned educators address the issue and come to a consensus. When drafting questions, consider what everyone in the room needs to understand and be clear about. Questions should be specific, objective, and open-ended. We recommend using the pronoun *we*, instead of *I* and *you*, as a way of framing the issue as a shared concern rather than a personal one. Making the questions open-ended helps elicit multiple solutions rather than a simple yes or no answer. Designing questions this way reduces the possibility that the person being asked the question will be put on the defensive, which is a particularly sensitive issue if the person has a higher status position.

The second-grade teachers who wanted clarity about how to use the standards, district curriculum, and textbook when planning math lessons first

**Key Question**

- What issue needs to be clarified?

**Key Question**

- What three questions can guide the conversation to get clarity?

needed to consider the outcome they wanted—the results they needed to move forward with planning. Second, they needed to create specific questions to get practical solutions, framing them objectively. Here are the three questions they decided to ask the math coach and district curriculum director:

> **Question 1:** How do we use the district curriculum map, math textbook, and state standards when planning math lessons?
>
> **Question 2:** How do we use the textbook with fidelity, even if the lessons do not align with the state standards students are supposed to learn?
>
> **Question 3:** If students do not master the math standard, do we move at the pace identified in the district curriculum map?

Just imagine the difference in the outcome of the Ten-Minute Meeting if the teachers used the following three questions instead of the ones they chose:

1. How are we supposed to plan math lessons?
2. Do you have to be on the same page at the same time every day?
3. Do you have to use the textbook with fidelity?

Teachers gain greater clarity about their main issue using the first three questions, rather than the last three.

> See Reproducible 28, The Ten-Minute Meeting: Three Questions (Sample).

## Step 3: **When Is the Meeting?** (5 minutes)

*Objective: Determine who will participate, then schedule a meeting*

Next, the meeting initiator considers who should be involved in discussing the issue. A Ten-Minute Meeting is much more effective if only a small number of people are present—optimally, no more than four. In the case of a large group of teachers having an issue, one or two representatives can be chosen to meet with the principal or coach and then report back to the larger group. Too many people may appear as "ganging up" on the person who is being asked to clarify. In addition, more than four people simply cannot have a natural conversation in the short ten-minute time period, so the others become just observers. Anyone vital to the conversation should be present, but extras only make the meeting less focused. The second-grade teachers mentioned earlier decided two teachers would meet with the curriculum director and math coach.

When the participants are identified, the meeting initiator finds a time convenient to everyone and schedules the meeting. In an email sent at least a day before the meeting, the initiator confirms the meeting and attaches the questions that will be the focus of the Ten-Minute Meeting.

> **Key Questions**
> - Who can help clarify this issue?
> - When can we meet for ten minutes?

## Your Turn

In thinking about how Ten-Minute Meetings can support collaboration and knowledge building in your school, consider the following sets of prompts administrators use to promote teacher reflection and cultivate conscious competence as they build relationships with teachers in a context of evaluation and accountability. Principals design three purposeful questions to promote reflection for instructional growth after a formal evaluation or walkthrough. Questions are chosen to create a reciprocal feedback loop, in which the question initiated by the principal as a result of the observations creates a learning opportunity, and both teacher and principal can increase their knowledge of effective instruction.

### Questions to Promote Teacher Reflection

- Where did students get excited and challenged?
- What worked well? Didn't work well?
- What teaching practices supported students? Didn't support students?

### Questions to Cultivate Conscious Competence

- How do you get students to communicate their thinking?
- How are you developing students' understanding of mathematical practices?
- What do you with students who do not understand?
- How might you use these questions in your school?

## Phase 2   Facilitating the Ten-Minute Meeting

**Approximate Time**   10 minutes

**Scheduling**   This meeting is scheduled at a time convenient for all participants—either before, during, or after school.

### Objectives

- Establish a rapport.
- Discuss questions.
- Synthesize consensus and determine next steps.

| Step | Document to Revisit |
| --- | --- |
| Step 1: How can we best set the tone? | Three Questions |
| Step 2: What are the questions we have? | |
| Step 3: Have we reached a common understanding? | |

## Step 1: **How Can We Best Set the Tone?** (1–2 minutes)

*Objective:  Establish a rapport*

The person who initiated the meeting serves as the facilitator. Begin with small talk as participants are arriving to establish a social, human connection. Use an invitational (as opposed to an interrogational) tone, one that welcomes everyone's thoughts and ideas into the conversation. Open the meeting with a statement such as, "Thanks for agreeing to this Ten-Minute Meeting. We are excited to get clarity on how to best use our resources to support our students' learning." Using an invitational tone requires modulating the voice to staying upbeat, yet serious. Conversely, an interrogational tone sounds like an interview or an examination. An invitational tone results in a reciprocal, two-way exchange of ideas, whereas an interrogational tone results in a one-way exchange of information, with one person asking the questions and the other person providing the decision or solution.

> **Key Question**
> - How can we set the tone for a productive meeting?

## Step 2: **What Are the Questions We Have?** (6–8 minutes)

*Objective:  Discuss questions*

The facilitator distributes copies of the Three Questions created in Phase 1 and articulates clearly, in as few words as possible, the purpose of the meeting. Participants consider each of the questions in turn, with everyone contributing his or her perspective or understanding. The facilitator should jot notes to document each person's response. Consider the example used earlier of the second-grade teachers trying to get clarity on how to use their textbook, standards, and district curriculum map. One of the second-grade teachers served as the facilitator and started by saying, "Thanks for agreeing to this Ten-Minute Meeting. We are excited to get clarity on how to best use our resources to support our students' learning. We know this is part of our Action Plan, and we need guidance to be clear about what actions to take. During this meeting, one question will be posed, and each of us will have an opportunity to respond. If we want to stay longer than ten minutes, the team decides this. Does anyone have a question about this process?" The group then proceeded to discuss the questions.

> **Key Question**
> - How can we get on the same page in regard to this issue?

**Key Questions**

- What is the synthesis of our ideas?
- What can we agree on and commit to?
- What actions can we take?

## Step 3: Have We Reached a Common Understanding? (1–2 minutes)

*Objective: Synthesize consensus and determine next steps*

When one or two minutes remain, the facilitator synthesizes the discussion and confirms consensus with the participants. Each Ten-Minute Meeting is different, and there are three possible outcomes:

1. The group reaches clarity on the questions, and everyone leaves with a common understanding to move forward.

2. The group stays longer than ten minutes to address all questions and/or to gain greater clarity on solutions.

3. The group schedules a follow-up meeting at a later time to reach consensus.

During the meeting with the second-grade teachers, math coach, and curriculum director, two of the three questions were addressed. The third question—If students do not master the math standard, do we move at the pace identified in the district curriculum map?—was not addressed. Everyone present decided this question needed an immediate response, so the group decided to stay an additional ten minutes.

## Phase 3    Following Up

**Approximate Time**    10–20 minutes

**Scheduling**    The follow-up occurs as soon after the Ten-Minute Meeting as possible, preferably on the same day.

### Objectives

- Compose synthesis statement(s).
- Share synthesis and next steps with participants.
- Plan any follow-up necessary.

| Step | Documents to Create |
|---|---|
| Step 1: What response did we reach for each question? | Synthesis Statements |
| Step 2: What did we agree to? | |
| Step 3: What are the next steps? | |

## Step 1: What Response Did We Reach for Each Question? (2–5 minutes)

**Key Question**

- How can I summarize briefly the consensus we reached about the issue?

*Objective: Compose synthesis statement(s)*

The person who initiated the meeting takes time to reflect on the discussion and review the notes taken, then composes a synthesis statement. Depending on the questions and how the discussion went, this could be one statement per question or one statement that captures the overall consensus of the meeting. Here's an example from the second-grade teachers' Ten-Minute Meeting with the math coach and district curriculum director.

> **Question 1:** How do we use the district curriculum map, math textbook, and state standards when planning math lessons?
>
> **Synthesis Response:** Always start with the standards, which identify what students are to know and be able to do. Refer to the district curriculum map pacing chart to identify when to teach and for suggested resources. Use the textbook as a reference and resource to plan lessons.
>
> **Question 2:** How do we use the textbook with fidelity, even if the lessons do not align with the state standards students are supposed to learn?
>
> **Synthesis Response:** Lessons must align to the standards. If a textbook lesson does not align with the standard, use the suggested resources in the district curriculum map instead.
>
> **Question 3:** If students do not master the math standard, do we move at the pace identified in the district curriculum map?
>
> **Synthesis Response:** Move at a reasonable pace, but no more that three or four days off pace. Focus on learning and using research-based instructional strategies that support all students accessing and mastering the standards.

## Step 2: What Did We Agree To? (2–5 minutes)

*Objective: Share synthesis and next steps with participants*

Next, the synthesis is emailed to participants along with a reminder about the actions to which everyone agreed during the meeting. The synthesis statements listed earlier were sent to all second-grade teachers, the math coach, and the district curriculum director.

**Give Me Five!**

## Step 3: **What Are the Next Steps?** (5–10 minutes)

*Objective: **Plan any follow-up necessary***

Next, consider if any follow-up is necessary. Follow-up takes several forms. In the case of the second-grade teachers, the math coach followed up one week after the Ten-Minute Meeting with an email to the team, asking about their progress; she also had one-on-one conversations with each teacher. Often, that is all the follow-up that is needed.

**It Really Can Happen . . . Insights from the Field**

Teachers pursuing a master's degree in mathematics teacher leadership were unsure of their role at their campus. The math coach had a specified role to support teacher learning in the classroom, along with organizing and facilitating teacher collaboration teams. Teacher leaders were learning, through formal coursework, how to influence change in teaching and learning, yet finding the time and structures to share new practices with other teachers at their campus was proving to be a challenge. They were working at a turnaround school with prescribed protocols for looking at data during a one-hour collaborative team meeting, and they were frustrated they spent the entire hour analyzing data without time to share new practices with the team. The teacher leaders felt that if a few research-based practices could be implemented, the result would be an increase in student achievement. They proposed that, during the data meeting, they spend thirty minutes analyzing data, then thirty minutes sharing new practices with the teacher team. The teacher leaders asked their principal and math coach for a Ten-Minute Meeting to reach consensus on the proposed change to data meetings. Here are the questions the teacher leaders devised, along with the resulting understandings that came out of the meeting:

**Question 1:** *What is the role of the teacher leader at this campus?* When we say "teacher leader" at our school, we mean the teacher leaders design a classroom with highly effective/exemplary teaching practices, open their classroom for public learning, and share new practices with other teachers. Time will be allocated during staff meetings for teacher leaders to share new learning. Teacher leaders will take responsibility for emailing new information to staff.

**Question 2:** *How can data meetings be organized so teachers have time both to analyze data and learn what to do differently to result in increases in student performance?* Data meetings can include time for analyzing and time for learning new methods of teaching. The suggestion is forty-five minutes for data analysis and fifteen minutes for sharing new strategies.

**Question 3:** *How can the teacher leaders and coach work more closely together to plan collaborative team meetings?* The coach and teacher leaders will meet prior to the team meetings and will codesign the session.

**Key Questions**

- What are the next steps?
- How can I follow up to make sure we complete the next steps?

## The Framework for a Ten-Minute Meeting

**Before the meeting, the initiator . . .**

1. *Identifies the purpose for the meeting.* As soon as an issue arises, an educator or administrator identifies the source of the problem or confusion, articulating it as concisely as possible.

2. *Develops key questions to discuss.* To keep the conversation focused on the issue during the meeting, the initiator prepares one to three questions that will help participants think through the issue and come to consensus on key points.

3. *Invites participants to a Ten-Minute Meeting.* The initiator determines who should be present at the meeting and arranges a time convenient to everyone. When sending the invitation, include the purpose of the meeting and the key questions for discussion.

**During the meeting, participants . . .**

4. *Establish a rapport.* It is worthwhile to spend a minute or two making social connections among participants, which helps set a positive tone and reinforces their common purpose as educators.

5. *Discuss questions.* The initiator acts as facilitator, keeping everyone focused on the questions so a consensus can be reached.

6. *Synthesize consensus.* The facilitator synthesizes the discussion, summarizing the points the group agreed on and confirming that everyone agrees with the synthesis.

7. *Determine next steps.* The facilitator notes the next steps to which the group has committed.

**After the meeting, the initiator . . .**

8. *Composes synthesis statement(s).* Referring to notes from the meeting, the initiator/facilitator composes a brief statement that summarizes the consensus reached by the group.

9. *Emails synthesis and next steps to participants.* The initiator emails the synthesis statement and next steps to participants so everyone has a record of the meeting and a reminder of next steps.

10. *Plans follow-up.* The initiator plans a follow-up meeting or some other activity to assess impact.

# Strategies for Success

Ten-Minute Meetings are practical, effective means of communication that can help teachers, coaches, and administrators stay in touch and on track all year long. Here are some strategies for ensuring their success.

## Frame Questions in a Positive Way

Questions should be developed using the positive assumption that all participants are there for a common reason: to ensure students' mathematical learning. Think of a positive way to ask a question. When seeking help in defining her role, a coach can ask, "How can I best support teachers?" rather than, "Is it my job to help teachers find their resources? Can't they find their own base ten blocks?" Asking an open-ended question allows the coach to express her concern without putting anyone on the defensive.

▶ Video Clip 5.2

To view this video clip, scan the QR code or access via mathsolutions.com/GMF52

## Developing a Vision in a Ten-Minute Meeting

As you watch this excerpt from a Ten-Minute Meeting, consider these questions:

- What do you notice about how the principal and coach contribute to the conversation?
- How do you think this discussion will affect professional learning at the school?
- What topic at your school would benefit from a Ten-Minute Meeting?

See the authors' reflections on these questions in the Appendix.

## Ensure All Voices Are Heard

If a Ten-Minute Meeting has more than one initiator, it should be discussed beforehand who will begin the conversation and who will ask each question. Constructing questions that are open-ended ensures there is discussion, not just a positive or negative response from the person being consulted. Invite each person to respond, striving for a shared conversation that is not dominated by any one individual.

## Research Says . . .

Evidence suggests that leadership practices that account for the largest proportion of a leader's impact is fostering the acceptance of group goals and creating high performance expectations (Leithwood et al. 2004).

## Minimize Conflict by Clarifying Roles

A Ten-Minute Meeting can make any school professional's functions in a particular role or situation more concrete and comprehensible. School-based work is multidimensional, requiring a combination of skills and activities that include managing a school; supporting professional learning; designing math lessons; assessing student understanding; differentiating instruction; aligning curriculum, instruction, and assessment for accountability; connecting with family and community; supporting the latest district initiatives; and a host of other commitments. It is not always clear which role an educator or administrator plays in some of these activities, so if there is any confusion, a Ten-Minute Meeting of invested parties can bring clarity about who is to do what. When everyone understands his or her role—and the role of everyone else—the potential for conflict is mitigated.

## Ensure Educators Share Language and Purpose

A Ten-Minute Meeting provides the opportunity for professionals in a school to discuss the significance of an issue, come to a common understanding about it in the context of the school, and dedicate their efforts toward a similar end. For example, during a Mathematics Vertical Learning Team Meeting, teachers realized they were using different terminology to describe traditional algorithms. When adding and subtracting two-digit numbers using the traditional algorithm, some teachers were saying, "Start with the ones place. Can you take the big number from the small number? No. So what do you do? You have to borrow a ten, add it to the small number, and then subtract. Thirty-two minus eighteen. Can you subtract eight from two? No. Borrow a ten from the three and add it to the two. What is twelve minus eight? What is two minus one? One." The teachers needed to learn common language consistent with number values and place-value concepts inherent in the algorithm. You *can* take a smaller number from a larger number. It results in a negative value. You say, *regroup* instead of *borrow.*" You say "Twenty minus ten equals ten," not two minus one equals one, when the values are in the tens place. Because these teachers knew using consistent terminology would help students, they agreed on which terms to use. Each grade-level representative then held a Ten-Minute Meeting with his or her grade-level peers to share this information and confirm everyone would use the same terms going forward.

**Your Turn**    **Gaining Clarity with Ten-Minute Meetings**

After a Ten-Minute Meeting, the professionals involved should be able to provide a common response when asked about the issue the meeting addressed. If there is a key issue about which there seems to be a lack of clarity, confusion about direction or language, or a misunderstanding, a Ten-Minute Meeting is the first step toward ensuring everyone is on the same page. Imagine two interviews.

**Interview 1:** A journalist from the local paper interviews eight people from a school: the principal, one teacher from each grade level K–5, and a math coach. The journalist asks each educator one question: *How do students learn math with understanding at your school?* Having a shared understanding of this fundamental question is essential to students' success in learning mathematics, and each person should have a similar response. If this happened at your school, would each interviewee have a similar response? If so, what is the response? If not, why not? How could a Ten-Minute Meeting help clarify this issue?

_____

_____

_____

_____

_____

**Interview 2:** A journalist is writing about the role of math coaches/teacher leaders in supporting students' learning math at your school. The journalist schedules interviews with the principal, math coach/teacher leader, and a teacher from each grade level. Three questions are asked of each person:

1. Why do you have a math coach/teacher leader at your school?

2. What does a math coach/teacher leader do?

3. How does a math coach/teacher leader impact student learning?

Would each interviewee have a similar response to the questions? If so, what is the response? If not, why not? How could a Ten-Minute Meeting help clarify these issues?

_____

_____

_____

_____

_____

| It Can Really Happen . . . Insights from the Field | At Wilson Elementary, second-grade teacher leader Ms. Reid had an idea for including peer teaching as part of her job-embedded professional development plan. She wanted to partner with Ms. Bridwell, a third-grade peer who shared the same philosophy |

of teaching, to understand more fully the second- and third-grade mathematics vertical connections. The school principal, Ms. Larkin, had other ideas for peer teaching. Ms. Larkin wanted Ms. Reid to partner with new teachers and/or teachers who needed to improve their math teaching skills so she could serve as a more experienced role model. Because Ms. Larkin was the principal, Ms. Reid perceived she had status and authority to grant the "final say." Because Ms. Reid envisioned powerful learning for both Ms. Bridwell and her from the peer-teaching experience, and imagined benefits to students, she decided to initiate a Ten-Minute Meeting with Ms. Larkin to see if they could come to a common understanding of peer teaching. The ten-minute investment proved successful because it allowed both Ms. Larkin and Ms. Reid to reach agreements on how peer teaching would be used to support professional learning.

## Validate Educators' Perspectives

In our experience, every teacher, math coach/teacher leader, and principal wants to be effective, be of value, make a difference, and impact students' lives in positive ways. Otherwise, why would a person get up each morning and take on the task of educating children in the context of high-stakes account-ability at a fast pace with multiple moment-by-moment demands? It's easy for educators to feel lost or disconnected during the high-pressure, rapid-fire school day. The Ten-Minute Meeting provides a structure that empowers all school professionals to talk about what is important to them for accomplishing school goals to impact students' lives positively. Anyone can initiate a meeting, and everyone at a meeting has a voice.

**Your Turn** **Design Your Own Ten-Minute Meeting**

Use Reproducible 26, Ten-Step Guide to an Effective Ten-Minute Meeting, to design your own Ten-Minute Meeting.

# Ten-Step Guide to an Effective Ten-Minute Meeting

## Before the Meeting

1. **Purpose:** Identify purpose for meeting.
2. **Time:** Request ten minutes from person(s).
3. **Questions:** Identify "Three Questions" and record.
4. **Share:** Make a copy of "Three Questions" for each person.

## During the Meeting

5. **Share:** Give each person a copy of "Three Questions."
6. **Record:** Document agreements, commitments to each question.
7. **Track time:** Keep track of time; the meeting lasts only ten minutes.

## After the Meeting

8. **Share:** Send a copy of "Three Questions" agreements to person(s).
9. **Take action:** Take action on agreements.
10. **Follow up:** Schedule a follow-up ten-minute meeting to assess impact.

# Ten-Minute Meeting Agenda

## Before the Meeting

1. Purpose: _____

2. Request ten minutes from the person(s).

3. Identify "Three Questions" and write them here.

    1. _____

    2. _____

    3. _____

4. Make a copy of "Three Questions" for each person.

## During the Meeting

5. Give each person a copy of the "Three Questions."

6. Document agreements and commitments to each question.

    1. _____

      _____

    2. _____

      _____

    3. _____

      _____

7. Keep track of time; the meeting lasts only ten minutes.

## After the Meeting

8. Send a copy of "Three Questions" agreements to person(s).

9. Take action on agreements.

10. Schedule a follow-up ten-minute meeting to assess impact.

# The Ten-Minute Meeting:
# Three Questions (Sample)

1. What is our vision of coaching?

   When we say coaching at our school, we mean . . .

2. What story do we want to tell at the end of the school year?

   By the end of the school year, the math coaching model has resulted in . . .

3. What are the coach's (my) tasks, duties, and responsibilities?

   At our school the coach does these things . . . Does not do . . .

# Tips for a Successful Ten-Minute Meeting

Every ten-minute meeting should:

1. Have three clear, focused questions that each person can respond to in ten minutes.

2. Be designed and facilitated by the person who initiated the meeting.

3. Start promptly—within five minutes of the announced time.

4. Include one- to two-minute human, social connections at the beginning of the meeting to build rapport.

5. Actively involve everyone present using Three Questions.

6. Move at a fast pace.

7. Meet a need that individual participants feel is important to them.

8. Lead to follow-up actions and result in participants personally committing to engage actively in that follow-up.

9. End on time, with each person's ideas to the Three Questions documented.

10. Leave participants feeling good, both about the meeting itself and about their part in it.

# Authors' Video Reflections

| Video Clip | Questions | Reflections |
|---|---|---|
| **Video Clip 1.1**<br>A Strategic Planning Session in Action | What elements of the session strike you as important or beneficial? Why? | Educators at all levels of the school system—central office administrators, principals, coaches, and teachers—are collaborating and engaging in conversations toward a shared goal. Typically, decisions about math initiatives are made at the central office level with minimal teacher voice. The conversations exemplify a learning system approach to building a strong mathematics program. |
| | What do you notice about how participants work together? | Participants are engaged actively and learning interdependently through collaborative conversations. They are not sitting passively, listening to one person talking at them. |
| | How does the session compare with meetings in which you have participated, either at the school level or the district level? | Most meetings are administrator led and are management focused. Usually, new initiatives are shared with a "to do" list to tell staff members how they are to comply and implement initiatives. Not all educators collaborate or have a voice during school- or district-based meetings. |
| | What happened in the session that would you like to see happen in your district or school? Why? | It would be great to see such lively, active engagement; investment; and ownership for success with district initiatives. I would like to see more of the collaborative spirit shown in the Strategic Planning Session. |

# Give Me Five!

| Video Clip | Questions | Reflections |
|---|---|---|
| **Video Clip 1.1**<br><br>A Strategic Planning Session in Action, Revisited | Identify and talk about what you see happening with regard to each of the following:<br><br>• Sharing<br>• Envisioning<br>• Goals<br>• Agreements<br>• Commitment | What stands out for me is the high level of educators' commitment, intentionality, and passion for improving students' mathematics achievement through strategic, purposeful, planning in a collaborative setting.<br><br>*Sharing:* sharing strategies freely in a safe environment and being heard by all participants<br><br>*Envisioning:* creating images of outcomes to be realized that improve student learning<br><br>*Goals:* writing clear outcomes in results-oriented statements<br><br>*Agreements:* coming to consensus through sharing the poster of agreements: vision, structure, actions<br><br>*Commitment:* all teams sharing their poster, with collective commitments for improvement |
| **Video Clip 1.1**<br><br>A Strategic Planning Session in Action, Revisited Again | Is there an obvious leader in each group? | Everyone seems like a leader in the group, as evidenced by their active participation. Each person contributes in some way—through listening, speaking, or writing. Information is transferred using inquiry and dialogue as a conversational style. |
| | Can you identify the principals, teachers, or coaches? | It is difficult to tell who is a principal, teacher, or coach. Each person seems to have voice and equitable participation. No one stands out as positioned above the rest, as is sometimes seen in school or district meetings. The principal isn't always the lead spokesperson when sharing the Action Plan posters; sometimes it is the coach or the teacher. |
| | How are educators talking with each other? Does there seem to be an equal amount of listening and talking or does one person seem to dominate the conversation? | Conversations seemed focused and collaborative; educators are listening and speaking to one another. No one person takes the lead and dominates the conversation. |

| Video Clip | Questions | Reflections |
|---|---|---|
| **Video Clip 2.1**<br>A Mathematics Content Learning Team in Action | What stands out for you about the meeting? | Teachers are respectful of each other. Conversations are focused on the mathematics and students' understanding of the math. Teachers, coach, and principal are working together. Each person solves the problem and all share their solution strategies publicly. Each strategy is different, and adult thinking shows differences from how students might solve the problem. If you don't know the people, it is hard to identify the role of each person. Educators anticipate students' entry points and strategies as they solve the problem. There is a knowledgeable other in the group that knows the math and can guide the mathematical conversations. |
| | How do you think teachers and students benefit from the discussion that took place during the meeting? | Teachers benefit from solving the problem, sharing their different solution strategies, understanding the math themselves, and anticipating students' solutions to the problem. Teachers' anticipation of student strategies supports the ability to differentiate for students and to ask guiding questions that lead students to making sense of their solution. |
| | Connect this learning experience to ones you've had. How are they similar and different? | Typically, a principal, teacher, and math coach do not collaborate about mathematics content. Rarely heard are teachers in professional learning communities solving a problem, sharing strategies with each other, and anticipating students' entry points into the problem. Professional learning communities are focused typically on data analysis and unit planning, rather than teachers learning the math themselves. |
| **Video Clip 2.2**<br>Building Knowledge in a Mathematics Content Learning Team | How did the group respond to the coach's question? | The group said, "Let them try." Ask the students if it is a good strategy. Students will see their strategy will or will not work. |

| Video Clip | Questions | Reflections |
|---|---|---|
| **Video Clip 2.2** (*continued*) | How did the coach participate? | The coach was a learner, contributor to the mathematics conversations and asked questions to push the thinking of the group. At the end of the Mathematics Content Learning Team, she asked the group what they would do if students started counting by groups (by twos) to solve the number puzzle. The coach's question caused teachers to anticipate students strategy so they could be better prepared with a question to push students' thinking. |
| | What conclusion about student strategy use did teachers reach as a result of the discussion? Do you agree or disagree? | The group wanted to encourage students to be experimental and to solve the problem in ways that make sense for them, not just do the strategy the way the teacher says to do it. Teachers became aware of the way they learned to solve the problem using the traditional subtraction algorithm, and realized students in second grade would think about the solution differently. The teachers supported the students' exploring to find out what is working. |
| **Video Clip 2.1** A Mathematics Content Learning Team in Action, Revisited | How did the facilitator encourage participation? | The facilitator invited participation by asking questions, and prompting each person to share his or her strategies and questions to push educators' thinking. At the end of the session, when the math coach posed the question about counting by twos, the facilitator asked the meeting participants what *they* thought, rather than answering the question herself. |
| | What kinds of specific information were shared? How did these specifics enhance the conversation? | Information shared included adult solution strategies and anticipation of student solution strategies. The adults realized their method of using the traditional algorithm was different from the way second graders would solve the number puzzle. Specifically, students would use the hundreds chart, would start from a number, and would then count on. Others would skip count or use a number line to start with the number and count up to one hundred. Understanding place value, and not just place labeling, was a big idea generated in this conversation. |

| Video Clip | Questions | Reflections |
|---|---|---|
| **Video Clip 3.1** <br><br> A Shared Classroom Experience: Briefing Observers | Who leads the meeting? | The teacher starts and leads the meeting. She begins by offering her lesson, learning targets, and flow of the lesson. This is a different approach than what usually occurs in a meeting between a coach and a teacher. Typically, the coach leads the meeting and the principal is not often present in a planning conversation. |
| | How do the principal, coach, and teacher interact with each other? | When the teacher began sharing her lesson plan, the teacher and principal listened. After the teacher finished, the coach shared her thoughts and probing questions about how students might engage with the math in the lesson. The principal was curious about what strategies students would use in the Racing Bears lesson. Instead of critiquing the lesson or offering the teacher advice ("Have you thought about" or "You might try this and do this"), both coach and teacher listened intently as the teacher described the lesson, and used a stance of inquiry to create thoughtful reflection. |
| | What is the benefit of having this type of meeting? | Benefits include creating a powerful support system that empowers teachers to change practices in their classroom in a climate of trust, respect, and collaboration. The meeting creates a "team spirit"— that coaches, principals, and teachers are working toward the same goal—and improved student learning. The meeting creates an equitable learning environment for coaches, teachers, and principals, where issues of power and identity do not impact true collaboration. |
| **Video Clip 3.2** <br><br> A Shared Classroom Experience: Teaching the Lesson | What do you notice about the roles of the classroom teachers? | The teacher begins the lesson and the coach adds a question. It looks like both the teacher and coach are facilitating naturally and fluidly the lesson collaboratively to support student learning. There appears to be no "invisible wall" between the coach and teacher that prevents learning conversations from happening. |

| Video Clip | Questions | Reflections |
|---|---|---|
| **Video Clip 3.2** (*continued*) | What do the principal and coach do as students work in partners? | The coach and principal are "hands-on." They circulate around the room, observe, and interact with students as they engage in the *Racing Bears* game. They ask questions to probe students' thinking and do not tell them the answers or ways they could get the answer. Typically, when either a coach or a principal is in a classroom, they are observing, critiquing, or evaluating, and are not part of the learning environment, providing support as learning partners. |
| | What connections did you notice between Meeting 2 and the lesson (considered Meeting 3 of the Shared Classroom Experience cycle)? | The purposefully designed lesson was taught as intended. Coach, teacher, and principal shared the same expectations and language for how the lesson would be taught. They knew the learning target, the role each person would play, and things to observe intentionally, such as student strategies used when they played the *Racing Bears* game. All knew both the coach and teacher would introduce the game. Students then practiced the game in small groups and went back to the interactive carpet to discuss their strategies. All knew what student responses to anticipate: counting by ones, using one-to-one correspondence, subitizing, and using strategic thinking. |
| **Video Clip 3.3** A Shared Classroom Experience: Reflecting on the Lesson | Compare the teachers' expectations for the lesson with what happened during the lesson. What did they learn about their students? | Because coach, teacher, and principal anticipated students' strategies carefully during the lesson, there were few surprises during its teaching. They expected students to use one-to-one correspondence correctly and to move the bears strategically by moving one bear the total amount or by moving more than one bear using decomposition of the whole number. They expected students to recognize dot patterns on the dice without counting by ones, and to choose which bear to move based on the number of spaces needed to get the jewel, not to move the bear based on its color. They also expected the students to keep an accurate count of the total number of jewels. |

| Video Clip | Questions | Reflections |
|---|---|---|
| **Video Clip 3.3** (*continued*) | What kinds of ideas were generated at the meeting? How will they affect students' learning? | Ideas included considering and naming the variety of strategies students used in playing the game—using just one bear, using more than one bear to get the jewel rather than moving all the bears. Strategies included collective counting, and decomposing (breaking apart or splitting a number), and keeping track of the count. Students recognized the dot pattern and did not count by ones. Another idea generated during the conversation was student engagement with one another and the importance of students working both cooperatively and collaboratively. Student misunderstandings were considered, such as lack of using one-to-one correspondence and keeping track of an accurate count. One suggestion was to use a ten frame to anchor the number. Students will benefit from the differentiation strategies and supports the coach, teacher, and principal generated. |
| | How do you think the collaboration benefited the teachers? The math coach? The administrator? The students? | The teacher was supported and benefited from ideas generated from the principal and coach. The coach was able to work collaboratively with the teacher, and not as just an observer of the teacher. |
| **Video Clip 3.4** A Shared Classroom Experience in Action | What do you notice about the relationships among the teachers, math coach, and principal? | Coach, teacher, and principal show respect for each other; their verbal behaviors build on each other's ideas. Their nonverbal behaviors indicate they are all curious and focused on the same goal: how *their* students are moving toward the learning targets of the lesson. |
| | How does the collaboration affect the teaching and learning? | Ideas flow freely among the coach, teacher, and principal. Each builds on each other's ideas, so they produce knowledge of practice. By exchanging ideas and methods for teaching and differentiating, the coach, teacher, and principal are producing a shared language and knowledge base of practice that will benefit students. |

# Give Me Five!

| Video Clip | Questions | Reflections |
|---|---|---|
| **Video Clip 3.4** (*continued*) | How might you expect this experience to impact future teaching and learning about fractions in the fourth and fifth grades? | Students are developing a part-to-whole relationship with numbers—3 and 2 are parts of the whole number 5—which is a necessary prerequisite concept for understanding fractions. |
| **Video Clip 3.5** The Power of a Shared Classroom Experience | What evidence do you see of a collaborative culture? | All adults are focused on the same goal: how students are learning the math in the lesson. It didn't seem that evaluation or judgment was present. Instead, coach, teacher, and principal were interacting, curious, and focused on listening to students and learning collaboratively about how the lesson and the teaching supported student learning. |
| | What do you notice about the interaction of the adults with the students during the lesson? About student engagement with the lesson? | The adults asked students questions to elicit their thinking. They seemed genuinely curious about what students were thinking. What the adults did not do was to tell students how to move the bears or show them a more efficient way. The students worked both cooperatively and collaboratively. They were supportive of each other, exchanged their ideas, and offered suggestions. |
| | How would participating in a Shared Classroom Experience benefit you? | Benefits include increased collaboration across the grade levels, greater knowledge of the math that comes before and after their grade level, and ways to differentiate for student needs. Other teachers can become aware that they do not teach in isolation, that what they teach at their grade level matters to students' growth and mathematical success at other grade levels. Teachers can begin to develop a shared mindset and knowledge base for teaching across the grade levels, build a repertoire of instructional strategies that increase student engagement, and devise ways to develop students' use of the mathematical practices. |

| Video Clip | Questions | Reflections |
|---|---|---|
| **Video Clip 3.5** (*continued*) | How would participating in a Shared Classroom Experience benefit you? | It would allow me to feel supported, not judged or evaluated. I would gain insight to my students from the different perspectives of the coach, principal, and other teachers. I would feel like I was part of a team and that "we are all in this together" for students. I'm not alone. |
| **Video Clip 3.3** A Shared Classroom Experience: Reflecting on the Lesson, Revisited | What kinds of evidence did participants discuss? | Participants discussed student strategies—such as use of efficiency, counting skills, one-to-one correspondence, keeping track, and decomposing numbers—and speculated on why students used specific strategies. Evidence was based on listening to students' thinking and observing them move the bears during the game. |
| | How did referring to evidence affect the discussion? | Sharing evidence allowed teachers to generate differentiation strategies, such as using ten frames to anchor the numbers 5 and 10 to support students greater efficiency with counting—that is, moving them from counting by ones to counting on. |
| **Video Clip 4.1** A Mathematics Vertical Learning Team in Action | What stands out for you about the meeting? | Coach and teachers are respectful of each other, as evidenced from active listening and eye contact with each other. The coach speaks from the student point of view. Conversations are focused on the mathematics and students' understanding of the math. Teachers try to connect the math in the kindergarten lesson to their grade level and adapt practices, such as writing. |
| | How do you think teachers and students will benefit from the discussion that took place during the meeting? | Teachers have greater awareness of how math content connects across the grades, allowing them to differentiate to meet students' needs. Teachers also had more awareness of pedagogical connections across the grades, such as increased use of writing, representation, and engaging strategies. |

| Video Clip | Questions | Reflections |
|---|---|---|
| **Video Clip 4.1** (*continued*) | Connect this learning experience with ones you've had. How are they similar and different? | I rarely observe teachers talking about mathematics content across the grades during professional learning communities. |
| **Video Clip 4.2** Building Knowledge in a Mathematics Vertical Learning Team | Which instructional strategies from the lesson do the teachers value and decide to use in their own teaching? | The teachers seemed to value more writing across the grades, and using models and representations to support students' conceptual understanding. |
| | What other kinds of ideas were shared that can affect teachers' practice? | Shared ideas included using learning targets, determining how to differentiate instruction, asking why students were making their moves on the game board, listening to student strategies, understanding how students were decomposing numbers, observing students' use of the number line, and noticing higher level thinking, strategies to support emergent bilingual students, how students develop mathematical practices, how to make vertical progressions, use of modeling and representations, and increasing writing in the math class. |
| | How does this type of discussion lead to improved mathematics instruction? | Teachers generate different strategies collaboratively that add to their repertoire. They also have an opportunity to see the strategies in action. |
| **Video Clip 4.1** A Mathematics Vertical Learning Team in Action, Revisited | Which connections does the fourth-grade teacher make to the math in the kindergarten lesson? | Fifth grade: decomposing halves, one half of four, talk about fractional parts; fourth grade: division, finding factors move four rows six times, or two rows of twelve; third grade: focus on fact families; first and second grade: modifying game to do addition and subtraction; practices for comparing relationships on number |

| Video Clip | Questions | Reflections |
|---|---|---|
| **Video Clip 4.1,** Revisited (*continued*) | How can these types of conversations lead to improved student learning? | The conversations shift the focus from "teacher watching" to "student watching" and bring greater awareness to listening to student strategies and thinking, which results in targeted, focused differentiation. |
| | What is a lesson you could share in a Mathematics Vertical Learning Team meeting that would be helpful to adapt to different grade levels? | I suggest sharing the lesson "Clear the Board" for students grades 3 through 5 from Math Solutions, because it creates rich vertical connections with multiple entry points by a K–5 team. For K–1 teachers, they can see the foundations needed for students grades 3–5, that are developed in the Counting and Cardinality, and Operations and Algebraic Thinking Domain. For teachers grades 3–5, they can identify student misconceptions, and identify how to differentiate a lesson for student mastery of math standards in the Operations and Algebraic Thinking Domain. The lesson ignites shared conversations about how mathematical practices can be developed by students during the lesson and across the grades. |
| **Video Clip 5.1** A Ten-Minute Meeting in Action | What stands out for you about the meeting? | Both coach and principal come to a consensus about three questions in a reciprocal exchange of information. Lacking was one person trying to dominate and convince the other person toward his or her point of view. |
| | Did the meeting seem like a productive use of time? Why or why not? | Yes, the meeting seems like a productive use of time because it allowed both coach and teacher to get on the same page, using shared language about the purpose of coaching at their school. |
| | How does this meeting compare with those you have had with key personnel in your building or district? | Meetings are usually lengthy, formal or informal, and not always structured in a way that results in a shared understanding of the problem of practice. |

# Give Me Five!

| Video Clip | Questions | Reflections |
|---|---|---|
| **Video Clip 5.2**<br>Developing a Vision in a Ten-Minute Meeting | What do you notice about how the principal and coach contribute to the conversation? | Both principal and coach communicate respectfully. Each listens to understand the other's perspective and point of view. Neither one tries to dominate; instead, they engage in a reciprocal exchange of information. The principal, who has the higher status role, does not try to dictate or sway the coach to her point of view. Neither seems to have an agenda to push; each wants to create a strong coaching support system for teacher and student growth. |
| | How do you think this discussion will affect professional learning at the school? | Teachers, coach, and principal will all understand the role of the coach in supporting teacher growth. They share agreements and understand how the coaching role will likely result in a coaching structure that supports ongoing, job-embedded professional learning that supports teacher changes and improvements to classroom practice. |
| | What topic at your school would benefit from a Ten-Minute Meeting? | The coaching structure, role of the coach, and how to establish highly functioning and effective professional learning communities would benefit from a Ten-Minute Meeting. |

# References

Achieve the Core. 2013. Progressions Documents for the Common Core State Standards for Mathematics. http://achievethecore.org/page/254/progressions-documents-for-the-common-core-state-standards-for-mathematics-detail-pg

Ball, D. L., H. Hill, and H. Bass. 2005. Knowing Mathematics for Teaching: Who Knows Mathematics Well Enough to Teach Third Grade, and How Can We Decide? *American Educator* 29(1):14–17, 20–22, 43–46.

Barkley, S. 2010. *Quality Teaching in a Culture of Coaching.* 2d ed. Lanham, Maryland: Roman and Littlefield.

Bryk, A. S., and B. Schneider. 2003. Trust in Schools: A Core Resource for School Reform. *Educational Leadership* 60(6):40–45.

Bryson, J. M. 2011. *Strategic Planning for Public and Nonprofit Organizations: A Guide to Strengthening and Sustaining Organizational Achievement.* 4th ed. San Francisco: Jossey-Bass.

Burns, M. 1998. *Leading the Way: Principals and Superintendents Look at Math Instruction.* Sausalito, CA: Math Solutions.

_____. 2015. *About Teaching Mathematics: A K–8 Resource.* 4th ed. Sausalito, CA: Math Solutions.

Carpenter, T. P., E. Fennema, M. L. Franke, L. Levi, and S. B. Empson. 2014. *Children's Mathematics: Cognitively Guided Instruction.* 2d ed. Portsmouth, NH: Heinemann.

Conzemius, A. E., and T. Morganti-Fisher. 2012. *More Than a SMART Goal: Staying Focused on Student Learning.* Bloomington, IN: Solution Tree.

Darling-Hammond, L., Chung Wei, R., Andree, A., Richardson, N., and S. Orphanos. 2009. Professional Learning in the Learning Profession: A Status Report on Teacher Development in the Unites States and Abroad. National Staff Development Council and The School Redesign Network at Stanford University.

DuFour, R., R. Eaker, and R. DuFour. 2005. *Closing the Knowing–Doing Gap. On Common Ground: The Power of Professional Learning Communities.* IN: National Education Service.

Dumas, C. 2010. *Building Leadership: The Knowledge of Principals in Creating Collaborative Communities of Professional Learning.* Department of Educational Administration: Theses, Dissertations, and Student Research, University of Nebraska.

# References

Easton, L. B. 2015. *Powerful Designs for Professional Learning*. 3d ed. Oxford, OH: Learning Forward.

Elmore, R. 2002. Hard Questions about Practice. *Educational Leadership* 59(8):22–26.

Felux, C., and P. Snowdy, eds. 2006. *The Math Coach Field Guide: Charting Your Course*. Sausalito, CA: Math Solutions.

Gallimore, R., B. A. Ermeling, W. M. Saunders, and C. Goldenberg. 2009. Moving the Learning of Teaching Closer to Practice: Teacher Education Implications of School-Based Inquiry Teams. *Elementary School Journal* 109(5):537–53.

Gallo, C. 2006. How to Run a Meeting Like Google. *Business Week*. www.bloomberg.com/bw/stories/2006-09-26/how-to-run-a-meeting-like-google.

Gamoran, A., C. Anderson, P. Quiroz, W. Secada, T. Williams, and S. Ashmann. 2003. *Transforming Teaching in Math and Science*. New York: Teachers College Press.

Garmston, R. J., and B. M. Wellman. 2009. *The Adaptive School: A Sourcebook for Developing Collaborative Groups*. 2d ed. Norwood, MA: Christopher-Gordon Publishers.

Gordon, G. L. 2013. *Strategic Planning for Local Government*. 2d ed. Washington, DC: International City/County Management Association.

Hall, G. E., and S. M. Hord. 2011. *Implementing Change: Patterns, Principles, and Potholes*. 3d ed. Upper Saddle River, NJ: Pearson.

Hill, H. C., and D. L. Ball. 2004. Learning Mathematics for Teaching: Results from California's Mathematics Professional Development Institutes. *Journal for Research in Mathematics Education* 35(5):330–51.

Hill, H. C., B. Rowan, and D. L. Ball. 2005. Effects of Teachers' Mathematical Knowledge for Teaching on Student Achievement. *American Educational Research Journal* 42(2):371–406.

Hirsh, S., K. Penscki, and F. Brown. 2014. *Becoming a Learning System*. Oxford, OH: Learning Forward.

Hord, S. 1997. *Professional Learning Communities: Communities of Continuous Inquiry and Improvement*. Austin, TX: Southwest Educational Development Laboratory.

Hord, S. M., and S. A. Hirsh. 2008. Making the Promise a Reality. In *Sustaining Professional Learning Communities*, eds. A. Blankstein, P. D. Houston, and R. W. Cole, 23–40. Thousand Oaks, CA: Corwin Press.

Jackson, R. R. 2008. *The Instructional Leaders Guide to Strategic Conversations with Teachers*. Washington, DC: Mindsteps, Inc.

Jensen, B., J. Sonneman, K. Roberts-Hull, and A. Hunter. 2016. *Beyond PD: Teacher Professional Learning in High-Performing Systems*. Washington, DC: National Center on Education and the Economy.

Johnson, J. F., Jr. L. G. Perez, and C. L. Uline. 2013. *Teaching Practices from America's Best Urban Schools: A Guide for School and Classroom Leaders*. New York: Eye on Education.

Joyner, J. M., and M. Muri. 2011. *INFORMative Assessment: Formative Assessment to Improve Mathematics Achievement, Grades K–6.* Sausalito, CA: Math Solutions.

Katzenmeyer, M., and G. Moller. 2009. *Awakening the Sleeping Giant.* Thousand Oaks, CA: Corwin.

Killion, J., C. Harrison, C. Bryan, and H. Clifton. 2012. *Coaching Matters.* Oxford, OH: Learning Forward.

Learning Forward. 2011. *Standards for Professional Learning.* Accessed at: https://learningforward.org/standards

Leithwood, K., K. Seashore, S. Anderson, K. Wahlstrom, and Center for Applied Research and Educational Improvement. 2004. Executive Summary: Review of Research: How Leadership Influences Student Learning. University of Minnesota, Center for Applied Research and Educational Improvement. Retrieved from the University of Minnesota Digital Conservancy, http://hdl.handle.net/11299/2102

Little, J. W. 2003. Inside Teacher Community: Representations of Classroom Practice. *Teachers College Record* 105(6):913–45.

Louis, K. S, K. Leithwood, K. L. Walhstrom, and S. E. Anderson. 2010. Learning from Leadership: Investigating the Links to Improved Student: Final Report of Research Findings. Learning from Leadership Project. www.wallacefoundation.org/knowledge-center/school-leadership/key-research/Documents/Investigating-the-Links-to-Improved-Student-Learning.pdf

McLaughlin, M. W., and J. E. Talbert. 2006. *Building School-Based Teacher Learning Communities: Professional Strategies to Improve Student Achievement.* New York: Teachers College Press.

Mullen, C. A., and J. L. Hutinger. 2008. The Principal's Role in Fostering Collaborative Learning Communities Through Faculty Study Group Development. *Theory Into Practice* 47(4):276–85.

Owocki, G., and Y. Goodman. 2002. *Kidwatching: Documenting Children's Literacy Development.* Portsmouth, NH: Heinemann.

National Governors Association Center for Best Practices & Council of Chief State School Officers. 2010. *Common Core State Standards for Mathematics.* Washington, DC: Authors.

Pearson, K. D., and T. E. Deal. 1998. How Leaders Influence the Culture of Schools. *Realizing a Positive School Climate* 56(1):28–31.

Pfeffer, J., and R. I. Sutton. 2000. *The Knowing Doing Gap: How Smart Companies Turn Knowledge into Action.* Boston, MA: Harvard Business School Press.

Reeves, D. 2006. *Ahead of the Curve: The Power of Assessment to Transform Teaching and Learning.* Bloomington, IN: Solution Tree.

Ronfeldt, M., S. Farmer, K. McQueen, and J. Grissom. 2015. Teacher Collaboration in Instructional Teams and Student Achievement. *American Educational Research Journal* 52(3):475–514.

# References

Saunders, W., C. N. Goldenberg, and R. Gallimore. 2009. Increasing Achievement by Focusing Grade-Level Teams on Improving Classroom Learning: A Prospective, Quasi-Experimental Study of Title I Schools. *American Educational Research Journal* 46(4):1006–33.

Schmoker, M. 2006. *Results Now: How We Can Achieve Unprecedented Improvements in Teaching and Learning.* Alexandria, VA: Association for Supervision and Curriculum Development.

Seeley, C. 2015. *Faster Isn't Smarter: Messages about Math Teaching and Learning in the 21ˢᵗ Century.* 2d. ed. Sausalito, CA: Math Solutions.

Springfield Education Association. 2011. 10-Minute Meetings. https://sites.google.com/site/springfieldsea/About-SEA/representative-council/10-minute-meetings

Supovitz, J. A. 2002. Developing Communities of Instructional Practice. *Teachers College Record* 104(8):1591–1626.

Tudge, J., and S. Scrimsher. 2003. Lev Vygotsky on Education: A Cultural–Historical, Interpersonal, and Individual Approach to Development. In *Educational Psychology: A Century of Contributions*, ed. B. Zimmerman and D. Schunk, 207–28. Mahwah, NJ: Lawrence Erlbaum Associates.

Van de Walle, J. A., K. S. Karp, and J. M. Bay-Williams. 2014. *Elementary and Middle School Mathematics: Teaching Developmentally.* 8th ed. Toronto: Pearson Allyn and Bacon.

Vygotsky, L. S. 1986. *Thought and Language.* Rev. ed. Cambridge, MA: MIT Press.

Wallace Foundation. 2013. *The School Principal as Leader: Guiding Schools to Better Teaching and Learning.* Minneapolis, MN: Wallace Foundation.

West, L., and F. C. Staub. 2003. *Content-Focused Coaching: Transforming Mathematics Lessons.* Portsmouth, NH: Heinemann.

Wiliam, D. 2011. *Embedded Formative Assessment.* Bloomington, IN: Solution Tree.

# Index

# Index

# Index

# Index